DR. JACOB YOUMANS

MISSIONAL TOO

The Trip of a Lifetime

III TRI-PILLAR PUBLISHING

MISSIONAL TOO

Tri-Pillar Publishing
Anaheim Hills, California
Website: www.TriPillarPublishing.com
e-mail: tripillarpublishing@cox.net

International Standard Book Number --13:   978-0-9818923-8-2

International Standard Book Number --10:   0-9818923-8-8

Library of Congress Control Number: 2013939608

First edition, May, 2013

Printed in the United States of America

This book is dedicated to Pastor Reno Johnson, Edward and Lamberta Gooday, and all of my friends in the White Mountain Apache Tribe. You all have supported me and trained me in countless ways. This book would not be possible without you! Thank you from the bottom of my heart for welcoming me into your family!

Contents

Contents *(continued)*

Contents *(continued)*

Acknowledgments

The following "thank-yous" are to people who have contributed to either *Missional U: Life As a Mission Trip* or *Missional Too: The Trip of a Lifetime*. This is our first time having "twins," so obviously there are many, many people to thank!

To Jesus, the Ultimate Teacher, who has pushed, prodded, molded, scolded, and refined me in ways that I am going to be processing for the rest of my life! Thank You for calling me to be on mission – and for surrounding me with an incredible community to be on mission with!

To the people of Our Savior Lutheran Church, Aiea, Hawaii; St. Paul's Lutheran Church, Orange, CA; and Concordia University Texas for allowing me to be on mission with you! You have all been so gracious in listening to these stories over and over again. Thanks for living them with me!

To all of the personal mission perspective writers: Thanks for your love and support! Specifically…

- To Matt Wingert: As I have been telling you for years, I'm excited to see what God's going to do with you! Never lose your passion for missions. You are most alive when you are on mission!

- To Cary Hoff: As of this publishing, you should be off to your next adventure in Vietnam. Now I've got to plan a mission trip out there! Proud of you!

- To Paul Stark: For the past decade you have watched the development of these books. Sometimes alongside, sometimes in prayers from afar – but always with excitement and passion! Thanks for always pushing and encouraging me to keep going – even when I feel like quitting!

- To Amanda White: As of this publishing, your next "around the world adventure" will be your greatest! Eleven countries in twelve months! Blessings on your travels!

- To Dave Talmage: You have been with me on more trips than I can count! You have been with me to more countries than anyone else! Thanks for always believing in a different way to do youth ministry!

- To Nick Miner: Your name may be "miner," but you were my rock during my St. Paul's years. Thanks for always being up for the adventure – and viewing life as one big game of "Risk!"

- To Ken Chitwood: I am so glad that God keeps bringing you back into my life! Thanks for helping to teach my Missional Leadership class at Concordia, and for always thinking differently!

- To Emily Eltiste: Now that you're a real live DCE, I'm excited to hear about all of your mission stories with your youth ministry! I'm excited to watch you raise up more missionaries!

- To Andrea Bolognini, the Concordia Texas legend – the first CTX DCE to do an international internship: Look at what you started! Thanks for believing in the "new guy!"

- To Nicole Seals: When I think about how far you have come in the last few years, I get goose bumps! From first-time mission trip participant to full-time missionary is unheard of! I'm excited to watch God use you in Australia!

- To Maile and Leilani Youmans: Your writing is getting so good! I cannot wait until you write *Missional U for Kids*! I hope you are as proud of your work as I am of you!

- To Lydia Humphries: You have been the answer to a decade-long prayer! Thank you for loving and serving alongside the Apache people! There are so many people that thank God for you being called there!

To Pastor Reno and the Apache people: I have spent more nights asleep on the Rez than anywhere outside of my own home. Thank you for allowing me into the Apache family! You have already taught me enough to process for the rest of my life, and I know we're not done yet!

To Ben Waldron and Daniel Wheel, for letting me crash your personal lake house retreat where I started writing this series! Thanks guys for your love and support!

To Paul Stark: I am so honored that you would write the foreword to *Missional U*. You are awesome! And you telling me that "reading this book is like sitting by the firepit back home" is one of the greatest compliments! It's been too long since we had a good firepit time. I guess I really only have one question for you: When are we going to work together again?!

To Ken Chitwood: Your foreword for *Missional Too* is absolutely fantastic! I am so thankful for your partnership in ministry! My students lovingly call you "the Lutheran Rob Bell," and I hope you see the huge compliment in there! You have an incredibly natural ability to make the simple profound, and the profound simple. I am curious and excited to see what God has lined up for you next!

To Peter Dibble: Thanks for another creative and eye-catching design! You make me look so much better than I deserve.

To Josephine and Andy Dibble and the Tri-Pillar family: I do not know how you do it all! You take my simple ideas and stories and painstakingly polish them up so they come out shining like the sun! And the best part is, the shining is a reflection of God's Son – Jesus – the Lord and Savior of the world! Thank you so much for believing in the *Missional U* series, and making this happen!

To my parents, Kim and Sandra Youmans, who from the beginning opened our home to be a mission outpost: Everyone was welcome. No one was ever turned away! Thanks for modeling all of this to me!

To Maile and Leilani: It is not a coincidence that in the process of writing of these books, you got to go on your first mission trip. I am amazed at how God uses you as missionaries now at ages 8 and 9, and I cannot wait to see what dreams He has for you as you grow! I love how seriously you take the call to be missional at your school and in the neighborhood. Jesus' love shines through you in all that you do. And I am so honored that I get to have you call me "Daddy!" I love you girls!

To my amazing wife Christy: When I first asked you out you said, "No, I have to go to a Mission Club meeting." I am pretty sure you were just blowing me off – but it's funny how 19 years later we're now on mission together! Christy, you have taught me so much about what it means to be missional. Your family's coming to faith story, that I am now a part of, has changed my life forever. I love you and am so honored to be on mission with you for the rest of our lives! I know you hate the cold – but can we please go visit Antarctica?

To God – Father, Son, and Holy Spirit: We thank You for the gift of life, the gift of New Life, and the calling to be Your missionaries!

Foreword

I remember the first "missionary" I ever met. His name was Andy and he wore linen pants. Really cool linen pants. I met him at a McD's in Rosarito, Mexico, and he was meeting up with our team before we went on to help build a home in a nearby *pueblo*. While I cannot remember what he said to us that day, I remember I wanted to be him. I wanted to serve in the mission field, I wanted to work with mission teams, and I wanted the linen pants. I wanted to be a missionary.

So, I bought the linen pants and started with homeless ministry in the greater Los Angeles area. I continued with short-term trips to Mexico and went to Hungary, New Jersey, Indonesia, Mississippi, and elsewhere. I served long-term in New Zealand and South Africa, and eventually was sent to the great country of Texas. Along the way I learned that being a missionary, being on mission, and living missionally means *way* more than wearing really cool linen pants.

Indeed, as my concept of what it means to be a missionary morphed, I found that I was not alone. There were others – in U.S. suburbs and Brazilian *favelas*, on the fringes of Indian megalopolises and out in the Australia outback – rediscovering the fact that everyone who is baptized is meant for mission, called to mission, and living on mission, even if they do not realize it.

The concept of what it means to be a "missionary," and how we are "missional," has been changing over the years. The notion of missionary is now recognized to refer not only to certain individuals but also to the totality of the baptized. The term missional was coined to encompass everyday mission and also imbues short-term trips on holiday with long-term purpose. Missional means being a missionary in global contexts *and* in your local community. Or in the words of Rev. David Kim of Houston, it means doing "glocal" work as the nations come to our communities and move in next door. It is discerning that relationship and mission are the purpose of the Father, Son, and Holy Spirit, one God, now and forever. It is recalling that because of this reality, mission is God's mission, the *Missio Dei,* and we are simply called to take part. It means that, in the words of Burundian theologian and activist Claude Nikondeha, we are "on a trajectory of transformation" in our churches, communities, and countries. It is educating ourselves, and preparing our heart and hands, for work of the kingdom – which God is already active in throughout our neighborhoods as well as places across the sea.

Jacob Youmans is just the right guy to give you such a missional education. He reminds me of my high school friends, Mario and "Hot Dog." The three of us did a lot of surfing in California, and one time we were up in Pismo Beach, up to no good. The whole trip was full of, "I dare you to __" and "I bet you're too chicken to __." And so when we came to the end of the pier in Pismo, Mario naturally dared me to jump off the edge. Inherently, I clambered on top of the guardrail and sat on the top rung. As I sat there, I wondered what it would feel like, how I would do it, if I would get caught, if I would do it with style (of course I would, c'mon)... And then "Hot Dog" pushed me. Splash. Before I knew it I took the plunge, was out in the ocean, and had to get swimming.

Through *Missional Too*, Jake is going to dare you to live life on mission – to dive right in. He will lead you to the precipitous edge where you will ask, *What would it be like if I lived life as a mission trip?* And, like "Hot Dog," perhaps Jake will even give you a shove off the edge and into the life. In fact, I know he will push you, because he is that great of a teacher, and a friend. But more than that, he will lead you into a deeper familiarity with missional living and guide you through the choppy seas and confusing storms to the point where you can concretely imagine what it would look like to be on mission right where you are, right now.

There are more than a few things about this book that make it stand out from others on the same topic. What follows is a quick overview of why you should not put this book down.

Jesus taught in parables. He shared stories to make points in tense situations. He told tales to poke, provoke, and push His people to see the Kingdom of God in their midst. His yarns spoke the language of the people and bore into real lives, reflected real situations, and often riled people up. Stories teach us. Jake uses stories of mission, from his vast experience, to poke, provoke, and push everyone who reads this book. He provides perspectives to guide the reader, and he does so excellently.

Aware that Jesus taught in parables, and that Jake does a pretty good job himself of relating didactic anecdotes, the reader learns that what is most important is not Jake's witty commentary but the essential playbook for mission – Scripture. Readers of this book will do well to note that Scripture is bolded throughout this series. This is not done on accident and I caution everyone to avoid the temptation to quickly scan over, or not read at all, the portions of the Bible that Jake purposefully includes. The Word of God is vital, and your education in missional living is incomplete, in fact it is invalid, without it. So when it is bolded – read it.

Another, and the most unique, element of this fine book is an intangible ingredient. Now, Jake is a self-professed "short-term mission junkie," but what he brings in vast experience is more than matched in wisdom. While he may always be on the lookout for the next opportunity to go on a short-term mission trip, a story of a trip he *didn't* go on is one of the most telling.

The first time I met Jake, he was not wearing linen pants, but blue jeans. Not holding this against him, I listened with intent as he talked about the importance of short-term mission. But then he stopped in the middle of his presentation and shared an axiom that shapes my life to this day. Offered the opportunity to travel to Sri Lanka to help people and communities in the wake of the Boxing Day tsunami in 2004, Jake declined to go. He said that to stay in balance, he had to say "no" to this great opportunity. That principle, "staying in balance sometimes means saying 'no' to great opportunities," is fundamentally true. It is a truism. It is wisdom.

More than his experience, which is prolific; more than his narrative know-how, which is exceptional; Jake will share with you his wisdom, and ask, challenge, and shake you to develop some of your own missional sophistication.

Now, you're ready. You are primed to read this book – to glean its wisdom and start living life on mission. So go buy some linen pants and hit the road with Jake in *Missional Too.*

Ken Chitwood
Houston, Texas

Introduction

Missional Too... What does this mean? It's not Missional *Two*... This book is more than a sequel to *Missional U*. It's a companion. If you have not read *Missional U*, you do not need to stop and go get it. You will not be lost or confused. But I must warn you – you will be challenged!

Your challenge, should you choose to accept it, is to live a missional life. Let me explain further. Live life as if it matters. Live life with purpose and intention. Live life... as a mission trip. I promise to quote *Mission: Impossible II* only once, but – "this isn't mission difficult, it's mission impossible."[1] To truly live a missional life might seem impossible. But as a follower of Jesus, you know that nothing is impossible!

When you live a missional life, you will encounter different people and different cultures. And as Tim Chester says in his book *Unreached*, "It is often our encounter with culture that first reveals to us our own culture."[2] When you live life as a mission trip, you learn who you really are – as you start to experience who God has dreamed you to be! This is one mission trip that is meant to last a lifetime.

The stories that follow are real, with real people, real lives, and real eternal significance. Despite some popular beliefs, hell is just as real as heaven. Living life as a mission trip is actually about a fuller heaven – more people coming into the true knowledge of Jesus Christ as Lord and Savior! Thank you for signing up for this "course" to become better equipped to be missional too. Let's get started!

What is Missional?

Welcome to Missional University! Let's start your training with the word "missional." The first time I heard this word, I lovingly yelled at my good friend Paul Stark for using it, informing him that he cannot just make up words. But now the word is everywhere. Here, in writing, I acknowledge that Paul was right and I was wrong!

I don't know if I have ever seen a bigger ministry buzz word than missional. As I meet people in ministry around the world, it's the word on the tip of everyone's tongue. But as I get into conversations, I hear many different definitions, ideas, philosophies, and lived-out practices. What does missional really mean?

Wikipedia® quotes the Oxford dictionary and says that missional means "relating to or connected with a religious *mission*." Now, I do not want to offend Oxford – and more importantly, Wikipedia – but I think missional is so much bigger than that. It's not a program or an event. It's a lifestyle – a way of life that seeks purpose and meaning in what others see as randomness and coincidence. And here is the Missional U working definition: *Missional means living life as a mission trip.* Every moment of our lives could be a moment to share the Gospel in our words and actions. Every moment. There is no coincidence. There is no accident. There is no off switch to it. Every moment can be a moment to share the Gospel.

Let me describe for you my Missional U training. I'm what some people have affectionately called a "mission trip junkie." I get energized from a mission trip like nothing else.

When I'm on a mission trip, I'm already planning how I can get back there.

I have led teams with junior high and high school students, college students, and adults. I've served alongside a truly wide variety of people and personalities. The oldest person I ever led on the mission field was a woman in her late 80s – and she carted bricks in a wheelbarrow all day long! And the youngest person was my two-year-old daughter who served with us at the Ronald McDonald House in Orange County, California. They had a policy that volunteers need to be at least two years old... Otherwise I would have brought her sooner! There are no age restrictions or limitations at Missional U!

By the grace of God, I have had the privilege of serving on short-term mission teams on every continent – except for Antarctica. (But people don't really live there, so I don't know if I'm ever going to get there!) My Missional U training ground has been the world. Please know that I'm not telling you this to boast in any way. That's not at all where my heart is. I never planned to travel so much that I'd get to every inhabited continent. It just happened. God opened doors, and I walked through them. Traveling extensively has enabled me to work in numerous multicultural settings, and with so many different missionaries. These experiences have taught me things I could not have learned any other way. In the mission field, like in the classroom, I tend to learn things the hard way. But I have learned an incredible amount during my travels!

Christy, my beautiful, wonderful, amazing wife, was born in Taiwan and her mother came to faith in Jesus through a Chinese missionary in Hawaii. My relationship with Christy is a large part of why I think so missionally! I'm just a lifelong, nerdy Lutheran boy. But I married into a family where missionaries have been used by God with miraculous results! Christy and I have been saying our next call will be overseas. Actually, we've been saying that since waiting for our very first call... However, God has not yet opened that door, at least not for a long-term call.

I find interacting with missionaries to be fascinating! They are all very different and yet have many similarities. I could focus on their differences all day long, but the biggest similarity I've seen in both short-term and long-term missionaries is they are very intentional about everything. They view every moment of the experience as an opportunity to communicate the Gospel. No movement is wasted. They live out the song, "Every move I make, I make in You!"[3] And everything is lifted up and surrounded in prayer – prayer support that is local and global, intentional and crucial. I haven't met a missionary yet who has underemphasized prayer. They also live in God's Word. The Scriptures are treasured and used not just as a textbook but as a guidebook.

Why can't everyday life be like that? I was tempted to begin this book with statistics on the state of Christianity in America. It's sad – no doubt about it. But others can give those statistics to you, and my guess is if you're reading this book you know that the situation is serious. You know that everyday life *needs* to be like a mission trip. You've enrolled in Missional U, after all! You know that the moment you leave your house, you are entering the mission field. In fact, many of you have a mission field right in your own home!

So this is what the *Missional U* series explores: *What would it be like if we lived life as a mission trip?* Is it even possible? Is it sustainable? What would it look like? Wasn't this Jesus' design for His followers and the Church all along? This book is your Missional University text book. We will go through stories I've accumulated from my "classroom of life," and you will be challenged to live out these lessons in your own classroom. The title of this series, *Missional U*, is also a play on words, where the dream and the goal is that by God's grace you will become a more missional "you." Like most good college courses, this will not be easy – especially if you take it seriously. But with a little patience and practice, you will be amazed at what God will do in you and through you!

Can I Get a Witness?!

To start, I want to draw your attention to Acts chapter 1. This is where St. Luke describes for us again (the first time is Luke 24:50-52) the Ascension account. Just before Jesus is taken up into heaven, He says in Acts 1:8, **"you will be my witnesses in Jerusalem, and in all Judea and Samaria, and to the ends of the earth."** As with all of Jesus' words, I believe He chose those words – and in this case those geographical locations – very specifically.

Before we get into geography, though, let's focus on the word "witness." Jesus tells us that we will be His witnesses. Eyewitnesses today are not always known for their reliability in court, but in an ancient Jewish court of law they were very significant. They were crucial to the entire case. In fact, there was no case without them!

Deuteronomy 19:15, written ~ 1,500 years before Jesus but still followed strictly in Jesus' time, says: **"One witness is not enough to convict anyone accused of any crime or offense they may have committed. A matter must be established by the testimony of two or three witnesses."**

Witnesses were crucial. Witnesses were the proof required to convict someone. And one witness was not enough... There needed to be two or three! So when Jesus says we are His witnesses, He is saying we are His proof! Together, we are the proof that He exists, that He loves, that He saves, that He lives, and that He's coming to take us home. Establishing proof for something is a major responsibility!

Let's view Matthew 16:13-17 through the lens of witnesses:

> **He (Jesus) asked his disciples, "Who do people say the Son of Man is?"**

> **They replied, "Some say John the Baptist; others say Elijah; and still others, Jeremiah or one of the prophets."**

> **"But what about you?" he asked. "Who do you say I am?"**

> **Simon Peter answered, "You are the Messiah, the Son of the living God."**

> **Jesus replied, "Blessed are you, Simon son of Jonah, for this was not revealed to you by flesh and blood, but by my Father in heaven."**

Jesus is preparing them to be eyewitnesses! He's showing them what it means to be "proof." He's teaching them to avoid the distractions and lies of the world, and to focus on the truth. I believe the question, *Who do you say Jesus is?* is at the heart of being missional. If you haven't wrestled with this question before – today's the day! Our words, and perhaps more importantly our lives and how we travel through the trials and realities of life, all communicate that

Jesus is the Messiah – the Savior of the world! Being a living-proof witness is a huge responsibility, but it also leads to incredible opportunities to help people know the truth!

Geography 101

Now, for the specific geographical locations, Jesus says **"Jerusalem, and in all Judea and Samaria, and to the ends of the earth."** Some have argued that Jesus wants this to be a "progression," like a ladder where you just keep going up and up until you reach the top. But Jesus does not say Jerusalem, *then* Judea, *then* Samaria, and *then* the ends of the earth. Others have argued that this is a list of "options," like a multiple choice quiz where one simply needs to pick an answer and stick with it. But Jesus does not say Jerusalem, *or* Judea, *or* Samaria, *or* the ends of the earth.

I would argue that **"Jerusalem, and in all Judea and Samaria, and to the ends of the earth"** is all-inclusive. It *has* to be all-inclusive. We're called to be witnesses – "proof" – in Jerusalem, *and* in Judea, *and* in Samaria, *and* to the ends of the earth. *Everywhere!* That's the missional life! It's viewing the entire world – home, near, far, and everywhere – as the mission field. It is seeing every human encounter and relationship as an opportunity to share the Gospel!

Some have argued that Jerusalem, Judea, Samaria, and the ends of the earth are convertible to city, state, country, and world in today's context. But as we look closely at these specific geographical locations, some additional concepts arise.

Jerusalem

Jerusalem is the holy city (Isaiah 52:1). At the time of Jesus' ministry, it's where the "in crowd" – the "Jew's Jew" – lived. In the Old Testament book of Nehemiah, we are reminded of the importance of the holy city. Nehemiah led the charge to rebuild the walls around the city to protect those inside and keep out those who meant to do harm. It was a safe place – a sanctuary from the cruelty of the outside world. I like to view my "Jerusalem" as my church, and, in a broader sense, all the people of God – Christians around the world who know Jesus as their Lord and Savior. We can be missional with Christians too!

To be complete, I view metaphorical Jerusalem as also including visitors who come to be with us for worship, Bible study, or similar spiritual activity, even if they are still unbelievers at this point, provided they are coming because of a sincere interest. After all – they have come to the holy city, as it were, and that is Jerusalem!

Speaking of visiting churches, I have the privilege of visiting a wide variety of churches in my current role at Concordia University Texas. Many of the churches I visit have a sign at the parking lot exit that reads: "You are Now Entering the Mission Field." Maybe your church has this sign. But there was one church I visited that had this message on *both* sides of the sign pole! So as people drove into the church parking lot, they were reminded that the church building and property are a mission field as well! So the question is: *How can I be a witness to fellow Christians and others who have a sincere interest in Christianity?*

Judea

Judea was a much larger area geographically, within which was located the city of Jerusalem. While inhabitants of Judea were mainly Jews, they generally did not have the same status as inhabitants of Jerusalem.

Metaphorically speaking, I view our "Judea" as people who are not Christian but are otherwise similar to us. Maybe they have the same socioeconomic status. Maybe they have similar ethnic or cultural backgrounds. These are people who are generally disinterested and possibly even a bit uncomfortable walking into our church, having relatively little interest in spiritual matters. *How can I be a witness to people who are like me except generally disinterested in Christianity?*

Samaria

Samaria is the name given to the Northern Kingdom, which was entirely separated from the city of Jerusalem. In Jesus' time, Samaritans were viewed very harshly by the Jewish people. They were not "pure Jews," being essentially half Jew and half Assyrian. Their hybrid status caused them to be viewed by many as even lower than the Gentiles. Samaritans were hated and despised by the Jews, which made Jesus' encounter with a Samaritan woman in John chapter 4 so powerful, and similarly His parable of the Good Samaritan (Luke 10).

We can view our "Samaria" as people who are in many ways *not* like us. Maybe they have significantly less or more financial means than we do. Maybe they have a different skin color. Maybe they speak a different language. Odds are, if they walked into our church, they would not feel comfortable at first. *How can I be a witness to people who are not like me?*

Ends of the Earth

You might think "Ends of the Earth" is rather self-explanatory, but let me explain it anyway. By now, you can see that I'm treating the regions metaphorically. So, continuing in this way, I define Ends of the Earth as people who have literally almost nothing in common with me, aside from our humanity. We share very few similarities when it comes to things like race, ancestry, culture, historical/political/economic context. These people might live right next door to us, although if so, they may be relative newcomers to our country who haven't had much time to assimilate. They may speak English, although it probably isn't their first language and there's a good chance they aren't fluent.

Whether we meet them on our evening walk in our neighborhood or on a business trip to a country we've never been to before, it really doesn't matter – because all over this planet, this third rock from the sun, there are human beings who need a witness who can "speak their language" (not necessarily with spoken words), love them for who they are, and share the grace, mercy, and love we have in Jesus! The Ends of the Earth could be at the end of your street, or it could be halfway around the world, but the call is to be His witnesses to these people. *How can I be a witness to the Ends of the Earth?*

. . . . .

All of the stories from the mission field will be divided into these four sections: Jerusalem, Judea, Samaria, and the Ends of the Earth. While I'm normally not a fan of "compartments," I'm doing this to show you the wide variety of mission and ministry opportunities that are around us every day. My hope and prayer is that they will inspire you to look at your world differently, and seek ways to be a witness as you live your life as a mission trip – wherever God leads you!

Traveling from the Ends of the Earth to Jerusalem

Now that I've given you the basics of how I view the four regions, let's talk about them all together. I've already given some insight into how people in the different regions relate to us on mainly a secular level: cultural differences, socio-economic differences, personality differences, etc. Let's get a little deeper into spiritual differences. Here's how I see the four regions from the perspective of religious context:

- The inhabitants of Jerusalem (don't forget, I'm speaking metaphorically) are Christians or are showing a true interest in becoming a Christian.
- The inhabitants of Judea are respectful of Christianity, and probably even consider it their "default religion," and yet they have no real interest in worship or living a Christian life. Many so-called "Christmas/Easter Christians" are actually residing in Judea. To be sure, most citizens of the U.S. – a "Christian country" – spend their life not traveling outside of Judea.
- The inhabitants of Samaria are generally opposed to Christianity. They may have a "default religion" of their

own – but this time it's non-Christian. Or perhaps they are simply apathetic when it comes to spirituality, even to the extent of referring to themselves as atheist if backed into a corner.

- Those who live at the Ends of the Earth are generally more strongly opposed to Christianity, often being a devote follower of another religion or strongly atheist.

To live a missional life, by the power of God we continually look for ways to guide others from wherever they are outside of Jerusalem into the holy city. And this should not be an occasional pilgrimage... The goal is for them to pull up stakes and make Jerusalem their permanent home.

In the ancient world, things were more compartmentalized geographically. Differences such as those I've touched on were more commonly accompanied by geographical differences as well. However, today's world is so much more interconnected. This provides us with opportunities the early Church simply didn't have. People from vastly different cultures and religious backgrounds than ours now routinely move into our neighborhoods, attend our schools, play on our soccer teams, carpool with us to work – you name it. Today, I can walk down my street, right here in our "Christian country," and be missional at the Ends of the Earth. And tomorrow I can hop on a plane and travel halfway across the world, to a "non-Christian country," and be missional in Jerusalem.

Like most people, I love to travel – except for one thing... It takes such a long time to get from here to there! *"Beam me up, Scotty!"* works on TV, but not in this galaxy. (Believe me, I've tried!) Being patient on a long journey can be tough. In a similar way, when we are acting as guides (and we ourselves are following Jesus) to folks who are taking their metaphorical journey from wherever they started to Jerusalem, we need to patient. After all, the Ends of the Earth is a long, long way from the holy city. Usually there are stops along the way in Samaria, but hopefully we can make it to Judea before nightfall. Once our companion makes it to Judea, that's when friendships can form and trust can be built. Come morning, the walls of the holy city just might be visible on the horizon, and feeling refreshed we can make it there soon. (Are you with me?)

Extra Credit

Interspersed through the *Missional Too* stories, you will find the *Top Ten Excuses Why I Can't Go on a Mission Trip*. In these sections, we'll explore ten of the most common excuses I've heard from potential missionaries. You or someone you know may be living in one of these excuses, and I hope I can show you ways to overcome any fear or hesitation and follow our God-given command to "go!" (cf. Matthew 28:19). Some of these excuses may sting a little as they hit a little too close to home. But hopefully you'll see how God can transform your reason not to go into an inspiration for yourself and others. People in the Old and New Testaments made excuses constantly – in fact, they used some of these very same excuses – and God still used them in miraculous ways! Even if you have an excuse or two, be prepared for God to work in you and through you such that, before you know it, you will GO!

In *Missional U* (the first book in this series), you will find another "top ten" list that I have gone over with participants on just about every mission trip I've ever led. I call this list *The Top Ten Excuses for Why I Can't Go on a Mission Trip*. This list has been created over many years of participating in mission trips and watching missionaries wrestle with these issues. This is a list of surefire ways to derail any mission trip!

But as you read that list of mission trip no-nos, be reminded that God's grace is bigger. Even in our sin and screw-ups, God still works! We humbly cling to the promise of Romans 8:28, **"that in all things God works for the good of those who love him, who have been called according to his purpose."** Even when we make mistakes, God still somehow works it for good in His miraculous way. While this list is designed to inform you of some of the potential dangers and distractions, we trust that God's Word will not return void (cf. Isaiah 55:11). God is still God, and He will still work in us and through us!

I am also very thankful for twelve of God's servants, each of whom is living an exemplary missional life. Each has been kind enough to provide a personal mission perspective (six in *Missional U* and six in *Missional Too*). I have had the honor and privilege of serving with all them on various mission adventures, and I am so thankful for their partnership and wisdom. I know their insights will be a blessing to you as you train for your missional life. They have trained in their own Missional University for years, and I'm excited for them to be a part of this course.

Geography 201

But before we get into the stories from the mission field, I need to bring up two more geographical locations mentioned in Acts chapter 1. Picture it. The disciples are witnessing the Ascension of Jesus into heaven. They are looking at Him rise into the sky with, I'm assuming, their chins on the ground.

They are wondering what's going on and what will be happening next, when all of a sudden **"two men dressed in white"** (verse 10) appear. It's safe to assume these are angels, even though we are never told specifically. And then they speak… **"'Men of Galilee,' they said, 'why do you stand here looking into the sky? This same Jesus, who has been taken from you into heaven, will come back in the same way you have seen him go into heaven.'"** (verse 11) Angels always say the darndest things!

Did you catch the other two geographical locations? **"Men of Galilee,"** the angels say. Galilee is their home. It's where they are from. I'm sure they have lots of family and friends back in Galilee. But I find it fascinating that they are reminded of their hometown right after they are told to be witnesses in Jerusalem, and in Judea, and in Samaria, and to the ends of the earth. Is this really a time to be bringing up home?

Maybe the angels are reminding them that everything has changed. What they have thought of as home is no longer their home. Their home is now Jerusalem, Judea, Samaria, and the ends of the earth. Being a witness, being proof, being on a mission trip, is too big a calling for someone just to remain in Galilee. The whole world needs to hear their testimony. For us too – we cannot stay at "home." We need to go. For Jesus, we need to willingly leave the comforts and confines of "home" to be His witnesses throughout the world.

The second geographical place? You may not have caught this one… Heaven! Heaven is geography. And for witnesses of Jesus – for all who believe in Him as Lord and Savior – heaven is our *new* home! By God's power and guidance, being missional is about helping as many people as possible claim heaven as their home. Being missional is about a fuller heaven. Being missional is about a mission trip where heaven is the destination. May it be so!

Dr. Jacob Youmans
Austin, Texas
May, 2013

Jerusalem

Introduction to Jerusalem

There may not be a more important city in the history of the world than Jerusalem. Geographically, Jerusalem is the ancient capital of Israel. It's the heart of the Promised Land that Moses only saw from afar (Deuteronomy 34:1-4). It's the city of King David. It's where Solomon built the first temple. It's the place where Jesus had His triumphant entry on Palm Sunday... and on a hill in the outskirts He was killed on Good Friday. It's an ancient city and a holy city to Judaism, Christianity, and Islam. The meaning of the name Jerusalem in disputed. Some argue it means "foundation," while others insist that it means "holy" or "sanctuary."

These definitions tie nicely into the metaphorical meaning that we will be exploring as well. Jerusalem is your church. Jerusalem is the fellowship of believers around the world. It's the "inreach" to the outreach we hear so much about. Metaphorical Jerusalem is big. If you want to know how big, check out the counter at: http://dom.imb.org/the%20 unfinished%20task.htm.

The call to be a witness in Jerusalem brings you to the challenge of "witnessing to the witnesses." It's the challenge of sharing your faith in Jesus in an encouraging and inspiring way with those who already know Jesus Christ as Lord and Savior. This is the foundation of the missional life. It's the call to witness to the holy people too. You do not have to go anywhere to be a missionary. You can be a missionary right on the church property! You can be a servant to fellow believers as much as to not-yet-believers.

As we go through these adventures in this section, I encourage you to constantly be asking yourself what *your* Jerusalem looks like.

On to Jerusalem…

Transformation

I love the beach! Having lived in Hawaii and California, I have been blessed to have the beach fairly close for many years. The continuous rolling of the waves breaking on the shore is a beautiful sight and sound. I could sit and watch the surf all day long. I have experienced the unique black sand beaches of the Big Island and the popular destination beaches of Newport Beach, California. But there is one particular beach trip that will forever stick in my mind – not for its sand and surf, but because it marked the beginning of a unique journey for a very special young man.

In 2005, I took my high school youth group to San Diego for a youth gathering. Just imagine 800 teenagers gathered along a beautiful Southern California beach! The kids were all excited to go. There was one particular youth in our group with incredible leadership potential. He was a little goofy at times, but I knew how well he could motivate a crowd. He was still young – only a sophomore in high school – but his potential was already obvious to me. However, I don't think he had realized it yet himself.

During the second evening of the youth gathering, this young man found a crowd gathered on the beach, and decided it was time to get some attention. He proceeded to "poop" on the beach, and then somehow lit it on fire. (I didn't even know this was possible!) And then he danced around it. I was not there on the beach when it happened, but as you can imagine, I heard plenty about it later as there were literally hundreds of eyewitnesses.

Now, I don't know about *your* youth group – but in ours this type of behavior was frowned upon! So needless to say, this student spent the rest of the trip right next to me at all times. He did not leave my side, and the moment we got back to the church, I arranged for his parents to come in with him for a "family intervention." During this quality time we talked about appropriate behavior and leadership potential. I explained that since he had a natural gift for influencing and motivating others, it was especially important for him to set a positive example. I tried very hard to be firm – but loving… and I failed miserably. It was obvious as we left the meeting that all the student had gotten out of this session was a sense of condemnation. After this, I barely saw him at youth group over the next year or so.

But something interesting happened while we were planning our next mission trip to the Apache reservation. This kid really wanted to go. I wasn't sure why, and I confess that I was more than a little skeptical as to whether it was a good idea or not. Not wanting to deny anyone the joy of missions, I allowed him to come on the trip. I am so glad that I made that decision, for it was clearly the right one. He was *fantastic!* You could tell something was really happening inside of him. And while he was still hesitant to come back to weekly youth group events, he didn't miss an Apache mission trip over the next few years.

Halfway through his senior year of high school, I needed to schedule another family intervention with this student and his parents. But this time, the reason for the intervention was quite a bit different. This time we gathered because the student felt a calling to be a missionary to Africa, while his parents were not excited about this idea.

About an hour and a half into the conversation, I called a "time out" and reminded them all just how far we had come in the past two years. In two short years, he had gone from "pooping on the beach" to wanting to serve God full-time as a missionary in Africa. This is called *transformation*. By the grace of God, it can happen to anyone – even someone who has been going to church their entire life. This is what being a follower of Jesus is all about. This is why we strive to live a missional life. When Jesus gets a hold of someone, you never know what's going to happen!

· · · · ·

Look through the Scriptures – when people encounter Jesus, transformation happens. My favorite account of radical transformation in the Bible can be found in the story of Zacchaeus. You can read about him in Luke 19:1-10. The name Zacchaeus actually translates to "pure and righteous one," which is ironic because we quickly find out from reading the text that he was just the opposite! He was a tax collector – no, check that – he was a *chief* tax collector. In that culture, tax collectors were hated and despised. (Feel free to argue on your own whether this phenomenon is different in our modern times with the good old IRS.) Tax collectors were very, very wealthy, and it did not come from an honest day's work. They cheated people – badly. They were allowed to tell people that their tax bill was significantly more than it actually was, and then keep the difference for themselves. Under Roman rule this was completely acceptable. Everyone knew about it but they were forced to obey or else face the full wrath of Rome. So then naturally, Jews who decided to become tax collectors were considered traitors to the Jewish people. They were actually "kicked out" of the Jewish race and no longer considered to be Jews by Jewish society!

Most people who know the story of Zacchaeus tend to focus on the fact that he climbed a tree to see Jesus as He was coming that way. The image of Zacchaeus scurrying up a tree is one that has been stuck in my mind since my early Sunday School days. Why did Zacchaeus climb the tree? He was a "wee little man," as the song goes. He really, really wanted to see Jesus – the Scriptures are clear there. But I think perhaps there is more to the story.

When our girls were young, our family used to spend quite a bit of time at Disneyland. One of our favorite parts of the Disneyland experience was the afternoon parade. If you've never seen it, believe me, it is fantastic! All of your favorite characters walk down Main Street and wave right at you! It's quite magical.

But, there is one rather large problem with the parade. People start lining up along the curb at least an hour before it begins. Since our family is not much of a sit-and-wait-for-an-hour-before-it-starts kind of family, we would usually end up arriving about five minutes before the parade, and then we'd have to stand in the back. But a funny thing seemed to happen almost every time. Inevitably, the crowd around us would look at my little girls, and seeing their eager faces and their rather short stature, the people would insist they be moved to the front to adequately see the parade. It's as if the community of Disneyland guests all said: "These little girls need to see this parade. Make room! Make room so they can see!"

I believe the reason Zacchaeus had to climb a tree was not simply because he was short. After all, there were probably many short people gathered along the roadside that day who wanted to see Jesus. Zacchaeus had to climb the tree because he didn't have any friends. He had to climb the tree because no one valued him enough to let him get to the front to see the Jesus parade. The community saw him as a crook, a thief, and unworthy of seeing this wonderful holy man as He passed by with His disciples.

Jesus, of course, had other things in mind! The missional life – the call of the Christian community – is to make sure everyone can see Jesus! Because when they see Jesus and make a connection with Him, transformation happens! And let me tell you, transformation is incredibly fun to watch.

When Jesus saw Zacchaeus in the tree, He invited Himself over to his house for dinner, and during that meal – that encounter with Jesus – something happened to Zacchaeus. He changed! The man who had cheated his own people out of huge sums of money said this: **"Look, Lord! Here and now I give half of my possessions to the poor, and if I have cheated anybody out of anything, I will pay back four times the amount."** (Luke 19:8) Transformation!

And what is Jesus' response? **"Today salvation has come to this house, because this man, too, is a son of Abraham"** (Luke 19:9). Jesus welcomes this man – the same man who was perceived as a traitor by his own people and kicked out of his race – into the family of believers. This is God's grace at work. No matter who we are or what we have done, Jesus welcomes us back into His family.

Jesus finished His response to Zacchaeus by giving us His job description: **"the Son of Man came to seek and to save the lost"** (Luke 19:10). If anyone asks you who Jesus is or what His purpose is, I think this sums it up pretty well! And if this is Jesus' job description, it also gives us a few important truths about our missional lives as followers of Jesus. Our job – first and foremost – is to be found! Jesus is relentlessly pursuing us, and He loves us with an unconditional and everlasting love. Our first job is to be found! But once we are found, our second job is to help seek out others. Our call is to make way so that ALL people can see the transforming love of Jesus!

Questions for Reflection and Discussion

1. What have you done in your life just to get attention? Did it work? Why or why not?

2. In what ways have you seen transformation in your own life? How have you seen transformation in the lives of others?

3. Who in your life needs to "see the parade?" How can you help them see Jesus?

Bump in the Road

While doing youth ministry in Hawaii a number of years ago, we took a group of about 25 eighth-graders to the remote island of Molokai. This particular island has a fascinating history, because back in the nineteenth century it was used to quarantine people with leprosy. So, it seemed like a natural place to take eighth-graders! Only about 7,000 people live there today, which makes it one of the least populated of the main islands. It is a beautiful place that lacks the touristy Hawaiian stuff common to several of the other islands. There is certainly adventure to be found there! While on this trip, we learned much about Hawaii history and got to partake in several adventure tour activities such as ziplining, camping, hiking, surfing, swimming, and mountain biking.

Mountain biking proved to be the most memorable activity by far. One young lady in particular simply did not want to go riding. But using my youth minister power of persuasion, I convinced her to go! I promised that I would be right by her side the entire ride, and that nothing bad could possibly happen to her. After we got safety instructions of what to do and what not to do, we got on the bikes. We all assembled at the top of a hill, and then started down the hill one by one. I was last to go down, with my hesitant student right in front of me in second-to-last place. As we watched the other students go, we noticed that there was a bump at the bottom of the hill that some students used to launch themselves into the air. It was beautiful to behold, and she even smiled as she watched her classmates having fun.

After a few minutes, it was just the two of us at the top of the hill. I looked at her, and she at me, and down we went. She was doing great at first, but then something happened as she got closer and closer to that bump in the road. She saw it coming, and started panicking. She tried to slow down, but instead of hitting the back brake on her bike, she hit the front brake – which meant she went flying head over heels over her bike, landing face first onto the hard ground. It looked as awful as it sounds. I've never seen anything quite like it. I jumped off my bike and ran over to help her, and noticed instantly that she was bleeding profusely from her mouth. Blood was everywhere. She had hit her chin on the ground so hard that the inside of her mouth split open – the cartilage at the joints that connect the lower jaw to the skull was severely damaged. I can't remember when I've ever seen so much blood in my life.

We picked her up, got her to the road at the top of the hill, and called the ambulance. They came and took her to the one and only hospital on this little island. There were literally no other patients there when we arrived. They took one look at her and called the surgeon. He examined her and said she could not fly home until the wound had been closed up. He told us that he had never performed oral surgery before, and that he was the only surgeon on the island. So, while he was performing surgery on her, he was on the phone with a major hospital in Honolulu as they walked him through his first oral surgery. I don't recall ever praying harder in my life.

After surgery, it got worse. She didn't wake up when she was supposed to. It turns out that the one anesthesiologist on the island was not accustomed to working with kids, and gave this 60-pound eighth grade girl a full adult dose of the anesthetic. I take it back – *this* is when I prayed the hardest in my life! I wondered for the first – and really only – time in my ministry if I had lost a kid.

Finally, about an hour or so after she was supposed to come out of the anesthesia, she woke up. She was pretty out of it – but she woke up! After awhile, she was cleared to be released. We all headed to the airport, got to fly first class, and brought her home to her parents safely. And today, she's happy and healthy, with a sweet scar that no one can see – and an incredible story that she actually remembers very little of!

As I have processed this event over the years and wondered what I could have done differently, and how this incident could have been prevented, one thing keeps coming back to me... The bump in the road. For some, that bump was a launching point, a stepping stone to bigger and better things. But for one student it was a stumbling block – a roadblock that prevented her from enjoying the potential of the adventure. How can one thing be so positive for some, and yet so negative for someone else?

. . . . .

In 1 Corinthians 1:23-24, St. Paul describes the message of the cross of Jesus in much the same way: **"but we preach Christ crucified: a stumbling block to Jews and foolishness to Gentiles, but to those whom God has called, both Jews and Greeks, Christ the power of God and the wisdom of God."** The cross itself is the ultimate stumbling block – or the ultimate stepping stone. To unbelievers, it is a fairytale or impossibility. But for those who do believe, it is the way to everlasting life. The very same message yields very different responses and outcomes.

God can work in a similar way through events in our lives as well. For example, tragedies in our lives that first look to be stumbling blocks can be used by God as stepping stones to help us grow. Conversely, some things that we first view as blessings or as too good to be true can end up becoming stumbling blocks for us, causing us to become complacent or lazy in our faith. How do we know the difference?

A key to understanding stepping stones is found in another of St. Paul's writings. Romans 8:28 states: **"we know that in all things God works for the good of those who love him, who have been called according to his purpose."** Even our stumbling, God works for good! Even terrible tragedies like Hurricane Katrina or the Columbine school shooting reveal God at work in the recovery efforts and ministry done of God's people. In a miraculous way these tragedies can show humanity at its best. I have encountered people who have overcome brutal diseases, cancer, malaria, etc., who can give an amazing testimony to a gracious God even in their sufferings. Some dear friends of mine prayed that God would use them to help provide a loving home for a child without one. They went through an expensive and lengthy adoption process – and through this course of events, the boy they longed to adopt was reunited with his birth family. While this was not the way they had thought God would answer their prayers, He actually did! There is no stumbling block that our almighty God cannot turn into a stepping stone!

I happened to see my student again several years after the incident, and her smile was as big as ever. After we hugged, we reminisced about that crazy day mountain biking. I teased her that she only really "mountain biked" for a few seconds, not a whole day – and she laughed. This event had become a stepping stone for her, too, as she learned that any situation can be redeemed. I asked her if she'd ever go mountain biking again, and her first response was, "Not with you!" After we laughed, she said, "Sure, why not? What's the worst that could happen?"

We have nothing to fear and nothing to lose. God will work all things for our good! That should take some of the pressure off when we feel like we are failing to live life as a mission trip. It also gives us the challenge to view difficulties and tragedies through the lens of stepping stones. God can use that bump in the road to His glory!

Questions for Reflection and Discussion

1. Do you tend to focus more on the stumbling blocks or the stepping stones in your life? Why?

2. How has God turned some of your "bumps in the road" into stepping stones?

3. Think of a friend or relative who's dealing with a difficult stumbling block. How can you help this person see their circumstances as a stepping stone?

What if We Quit Everything and Just Did This?

A good mission trip blesses the server as much as those being served. It usually takes awhile for this concept to hit people, but I've seen it happen just about every time. Mission trips force you to ask the *Why me?* question. *Why do I have all these blessings and advantages? Why do I have my family, my house, my education, my upbringing, my culture, my financial resources?* Especially in our American context, *Why me?* is a crucial question that we should all ask ourselves at some point.

I was talking with a citizen of another country who recently visited the United States for the first time. I asked him if he thought he could live permanently in an American context. He said that he and his wife discussed it quite a bit after their visit. They had no plans to move, but they were going through the thought experiment of whether they could live in the States. And their conclusion? No. Why? Because they felt that all the wealth and the waste would make them uncomfortable. Now, we shouldn't apologize for being American and for being blessed. But all of our blessings do force us to ask that question, *Why me?*

Back in the early 2000s, I took a small group on a short mission trip to serve a church in Inglewood, California. The area we went to was predominantly African-American, and the students in our group were not. For many of us, Inglewood seemed like a far off and distant land, even though it was actually only forty miles away from our homes in Orange County. The socioeconomic differences between those who were serving, and those being served, were vast.

This was our first such trip, but certainly not the last. We ended up going at least once a year for the rest of my time in California. This was a relatively small group, as there were only twelve of us altogether: ten high school students and two adult chaperones. We were only staying one night and working two full days. But the church had no showers or housing facilities available. We slept on the concrete floor, and readily accepted the fact that we were just going to be dirty and smelly for a few days.

During the course of the first day, one of our students seemed to have disappeared. When he didn't show up for lunch, I knew something was really odd because this particular student *never* skipped lunch, let alone a work break! Knowing that it's not a good thing when a kid goes missing in Inglewood, we sent a few students to look for him. A while later, they came and got me, telling me that they found him in the church sanctuary – mopping. The grounds of the church property were rather extensive, and with the weather usually so beautiful in Southern California, the buildings were not connected by inside hallways. So it was possible for nobody to have seen him even though he was on site the entire time. This young man had taken it upon himself to mop the entire floor of the sanctuary. He was sweaty and dirty from head to toe. When I asked him if he had been mopping all this time, he just looked at me and smiled from ear to ear. He was exhausted. But he had done a wonderful job of serving and giving of himself. Even though he didn't say much of anything, I could tell that something was going on inside of him. Something was changing. He was beginning the transformation from selfish to selfless.

We all slept very well that night. Through the discussions and processing we did as a group, I could see some of the students were asking the *Why me?* question. The place we were serving wasn't even around the world – it was just forty miles down the road! – and yet the question still hit them. The next day we continued our physical labor, and everyone worked hard. During the last hour or so of our time at the church, the mopping student and I were throwing things away in an already overflowing dumpster. It was just the two of us, and he was still very quiet. He was very focused on getting all of the trash into the bin when he suddenly turned to me and asked, "Jake, don't you get the feeling that if we quit everything else and just did *this*, we could change the world?" I do not even recall my answer – even though I'm sure I gave one. But through the course of a couple of days in Inglewood, the question of *Why me?* had developed into a new question: *Now what?* Now that we know how blessed we are, we can't just sit and revel in those blessings. We've got to do something with them! We've got to change the world!

. . . . .

God loves the world so much that He sent Jesus. And Jesus so loved the world that He lived the perfect life that you and I could never live, died the brutal death that you and I would never want to die, rose again under His own power to conquer sin, death, and the devil, and lives and reigns in heaven bringing home all who believe in Him. God also so loved the world that He sent the Holy Spirit – the power-bringer – who empowers us to change the world.

As Jesus was praying all alone in the garden, right before He was arrested and the night before He was put to death, He prayed these words: **"As you sent me into the world, I have sent them into the world."** (John 17:18) Jesus has sent *us* into the world to change the world – to continue the mission that He started. The answer to *Now what?* has got to be – *Let's change the world!*

In the movie *Savages*, directed by Oliver Stone, the two main characters are drug dealers who have made an incredible living for themselves. One is a former soldier who has been hardened by the world, and the other is a philanthropist who wants to use the money he's made from the drug game to make a positive difference in the world. He's exploring getting laptops into the hands of kids in Africa for their educational needs. He has a Robin Hood-type of mentality, and wants to get out of the drug business. As he's explaining his idea to his partner – telling him that they have the ability to really do some good and to change the world – his partner's cold, unemotional response is: "The problem is, the *world* changes *you*."[4] To this, he has no response. And through the course of the movie, both friends partake in unspeakable acts of violence because the world has changed them. What do you think? Does the world have the power to change you?

Make no mistake – the world *does* have the power to change you. Watch the nightly news or read the morning paper, and you'll see plenty of stories of people who have been changed by the world. But hear the words of St. John in 1 John 4:4 – **"You, dear children, are from God and have overcome them, because the one who is in you is greater than the one who is in the world."** Greater is He who is in you than the one who is in the world! Because you belong to God, you already have everything you need to change the world!

You don't have to think *big* to change the world. Instead, think *doable*. Mopping a church is doable. So is handing out food to the hungry, visiting someone in the hospital, shoveling snow for an elderly neighbor, or picking up trash in the neighborhood. The world may tell us, *Don't sweat the small stuff!* – but God is in the small stuff! If everyone did the small stuff, the world would change in amazing ways! Love in action, whether big or small, can make a huge difference.

So – now what? What are you going to do? Who are you going to be? How are you going to change the world?

Questions for Reflection and Discussion

1. When you reflect on the abundance of blessings in your life, do you ever find yourself asking the question, *Why me?*

2. Have you reached the point of asking *Now what?* How are you answering this question?

3. What does "change the world" mean to you?

4. What is something you could "quit" in order to devote more time to changing the world?

The Funeral

January 2012 – just four months shy of his 90th birthday – my maternal grandfather passed away. My grandfather, Erwin J. Geiger, was an amazing man. He had a huge impact on my life, and he taught me so many things. He taught me how to ride a bike, how to play chess, and how to tell a story. He taught me that it's OK to tell a joke over and over again – it will always be funny! My grandfather taught me that you can be an artist *and* a scientist. He taught me that in order to really understand the world, you have to *travel* around the world. He taught me, by the way he lived his life, the priorities of God / family / country. He was my living history book. My hero. My patriarch.

My grandmother asked if I would preach at the funeral. I don't know how it works in your family, but when Grandma asks you to do anything, you say: "Yes!" I was truly honored to be asked, and very excited to serve and remember him in this way. The funeral was scheduled for 4:00 P.M. on a Wednesday in Orlando, Florida, and due to my teaching and travel schedule, I could not leave Texas until 5:30 A.M. that morning. But I knew this should get me into Orlando at 11:00 A.M., with plenty of time to spare.

But things didn't work out that way at all. There was a huge thunderstorm that morning, and I was stuck in Houston. They shut down the Houston airport, and as hard as I tried, I could not get a flight out that would get me to Orlando in time for the funeral. At 11:00 A.M., I finally had to call my mother – who assumed by this time that I had already landed in Orlando – and break the news to her that I was not going to be able to be there in time for the funeral. She just said: "No Jacob! You *have* to be here!"

But I couldn't be there, and there was absolutely nothing I could do. Now I am not really one to cry – and I certainly do not make a habit of crying in public – but at that moment, I lost it. I just started crying. I cried right there in front of the nice ticketing agent who tried so hard to help me. I felt helpless. People kept calling me with ideas of things to try in order to get there in time, but nothing worked. But then my cousin James had a fantastic suggestion. He said I should find someone with an iPhone® (I did not own one at the time, but you better believe I got one after this experience!) and ask them to record a video of me giving my sermon. Then we could e-mail it to the church and they would be able to show it on the big screen during the funeral.

The entire airport had been shut down for several hours, and we were told it would be several more before even one flight got out. All of this made the clientele of the airport rather grumpy, as everyone's travel plans were now completely disrupted. I happened to be sitting next to one particularly grumpy yet chatty man who was using plenty of colorful language to describe his frustration with the delay.

After my cousin gave me the idea of an iPhone recording, I explained my situation to this man and asked him if he would be kind enough to record my sermon on his iPhone and then send the video file to the church. He agreed, and graciously filmed my sermon while I sat there and preached from my seat in the middle of a bustling and noisy airport. The sermon itself was only about ten minutes long, but even so, my "director" kept giving me hand signals to move things along as quickly as possible because he was not sure how long his low battery would last. After a few minutes, people started gathering to watch us, wondering what we were doing. But I tuned them out and focused on the camera as I delivered my heartfelt message, honoring Grandpa and fulfilling my promise to Grandma.

Interestingly enough, this gentleman's colorful language ceased as he attentively listened to my message about life and death and new life in Jesus. By the end, his grumpiness seemed to disappear. As soon as we were done taping, he started to send the video file to the church – but it wouldn't send. There were so many people trying to access the Internet at once that it was moving very slowly, and we could not send out the video, which was a fairly large file. The video was stuck on his phone. Failure yet again.

Later, as I parted ways with my new friend, he assured me that he would continue trying to send that video. But it was never received by the church. As I look back at that moment, I still wonder why God would allow me to miss the funeral, and not be able to deliver my message. I wonder how He would somehow work good through this whole situation. And my mind keeps going back to my iPhone videographer. Perhaps all of this was to share the love and grace of Jesus with him. Maybe the message was actually delivered to the person who needed to hear it the most that day. Who knows how God used our time together to bless him. I had certainly seen some small changes in him during our few hours together. What if God allowed me to experience all of the messiness of that experience just to reach him? Only God knows. But it wouldn't be unlike Him! That's the story of the resurrection – good coming out of tragedy and death. What if

Grandpa's death led to this stranger's resurrection? Even though I will most likely never know in this lifetime – it is certainly my prayer!

. . . . .

For the funeral service, my family chose to reflect on Ecclesiastes 3:1-8. I invite you to read through it. It's all about God's timing for things. Everything has a season. Everything has a time. We only have so much time here on this earth, and we have to make the most of it. Is anything worse than wasted time? Think of all the minutes, hours, days, and years in your life that have already passed. Have you made the most of them? You can never get them back!

But I think we need to continue on to verse 9 of chapter 3, where King Solomon – the wisest man the world has ever known – asks the question: **"What do workers gain from their toil?"** Interesting question. What do we gain? I will be so bold as to answer on behalf of my grandfather's life: First and foremost he gained the joy of telling others about Jesus' promise of eternal life. That promise is not given to us on the basis of our own "toil" or anything we have done, but on what Jesus did for each of us on the cross and through the resurrection. Because Jesus conquered death, so did my grandpa. He's gained eternal life. And all those who believe in Jesus will one day be reunited in heaven forever. What a humbling idea that our "toiling" – our living life as a mission trip – could actually lead others to eternal life! It really makes it not feel like toiling when we have an eternal perspective!

It's pretty humbling to realize that God can use us even when we don't realize it. To really embrace this idea of life as a mission trip, we need to understand that any interaction with another human being has the potential for eternal significance. The mission field is everywhere and anywhere we happen to be! And sometimes the very things that mess up our plans and our schedules actually fit into His good and gracious plan. It's certainly something to think about, the next time you are stuck in a place you do not want to be! Maybe God has a greater purpose.

Questions for Reflection and Discussion

1. Have you ever lost someone close to you? Share a specific way in which you honored this person after they passed away.

2. Where is the most bizarre or unusual place you've found yourself in the "mission field?"

3. What have you gained from your "toil?" Do you think you are making a lasting impact on others through your words and actions?

Top Ten Excuses for Why I Can't Go on a Mission Trip – #10 and #9

While there are certainly hundreds if not thousands of excuses for why we can't go on a mission trip, I have assembled for you the top ten. I've heard all of these excuses on multiple occasions from a wide variety of people. Now, I'm not doubting their sincerity (or yours, for that matter!). My point in sharing this list is not to judge, but to encourage. I want to challenge you to look at your own doubts, fears, and hesitations, and not let these things stand in your way. What's funny is that God has been hearing these exact same excuses from His people for thousands of years! We see them all throughout Scripture. But God has called us to be His witnesses, and He will help us overcome any stumbling block!

. . . . .

"I'm Too Old"

This is a good excuse for many things in life. We need to slow down a bit as we get older. It's a fact of life. But in a society where people are living longer and are more productive in older age, it really makes you think about the saying, "Age is an attitude, not a number." Is anyone really too old? Since Jesus still has you here – I'd say He's not done with you yet!

One of my favorite Bible stories related to the "too old" excuse is God telling Abraham and Sarah that late in age they would give birth to a son (Genesis 17:1-17). Abraham (Genesis 17:17) and Sarah (Genesis 18:9-15) both laughed so hard that when she eventually had that promised baby, they had to name their child "laughter" (Genesis 17:19 and 21:1-6)! They may have thought they were too old – but God had a different plan!

With age comes wisdom and experience. Those are two great things to bring on a mission trip! What a witness it is when someone who is later in life does something they're considered "too old" for! George H.W. Bush jumped out of an airplane for his 80th birthday. Brett Favre threw touchdown passes into his forties. Clint Eastwood won an Oscar for Best Director at age 74! They inspired people. And you can too, by going on a mission trip – no matter how old you are!

"I'm Too Young"

Now, for travel to certain countries, one wants to be wise when it comes to how young participants should be. But, by and large, there really isn't an age that is too young. I started taking my kids on day-long service events at the ripe old age of 2. I took them on their first week-long mission trip at ages 8 and 9. They were very hardworking and inspiring in their service. I was so proud of them!

The "too young" excuse is addressed in Scripture as well. St. Paul says to his young missionary protégé, Timothy, **"Don't let anyone look down on you because you are young, but set an example for the believers in speech, in conduct, in love, in faith and in purity."** (1 Timothy 4:12) Young people can be incredible examples. In fact, young people can inspire the older and wiser to get involved too! After all, Jesus commands us to have faith like a child (Luke 18:15-17). So, you really can't be too young!

Personal Mission Perspective

A Wing, a Prayer, and a Paper Airplane
by Rev. Paul Stark

My first-ever mission trip was during college, to an orphanage in the hills just outside of Tijuana, Mexico. I didn't speak the language. I didn't have any theological training. To be honest, I didn't even have a great desire to be there. I'd been asked by friends to go, and because I wasn't assertive enough at that point in my life to decline their invitation, I reluctantly agreed to give up a weekend and head south of the border with them.

Once we arrived at the orphanage, my worst fears came true: I was an absolute fish out of water. I had no idea what to do. We had no agenda for the day, there was no list of projects to be completed, and there was nowhere to slink off and hide. The only thing in evidence there on that dusty hillside amidst the dilapidated buildings were eyes – pairs and pairs of big, brown, earnest, hopeful, expectant eyes – all staring up at me, waiting for who knows what.

We'd brought along some copy paper and crayons so we could color with the kids, but I was a terrible, impatient artist and I couldn't draw my way out of a paper bag. Suddenly, however, I remembered the one thing I *could* do with paper, and in an act of sheer desperation, I did it. I began folding the sheets into paper airplanes. When the first one left my hand and went soaring through the air, there was an audible gasp from the children. They'd never seen such a thing before. And just like that, everything clicked. All was well. The language barrier prevented us from conversing much as the hours passed, but all through the day those planes flew back and forth across the dingy, trash-strewn courtyard. That, combined with the laughter, the hugs, and the high-fives, was communication enough for me.

That night at dinner, the orphanage's house mother gave devotions, and there was an interpreter to share in English what she was speaking in Spanish. As she stood, I noticed that she held in her hand one of the used up, slightly crumpled planes we had made earlier in the day. She began to tell us how, as a young girl, her dream had been to fly to distant lands in a real plane so she could tell others about the love of Jesus. Her dream never came true, she said, because God had children right there in Mexico who needed her to share Jesus with them. "But I have a new dream," she continued with a smile on her face. "My dream is that some of you will fly for me. Some of you will grow up, get on a plane, and fly all around the world telling people of God's love and forgiveness in our Savior." When she asked how many children would like to tell others about Christ in that way, a sea of hands shot up, a chorus of excited chatter filled the room, and a wave of joyful eagerness swept across the faces of dozens of boys and girls completely taken with the idea. It was like they were catching the dream right then and there, owning it, committing to it in their hearts. As the house mother prayed aloud that night, she asked the Lord to raise up from that very group of children missionaries who would one day go into all the world and share the Good News. It was an awesome moment, and I was left humbled by what God had done through a hapless, reluctant college kid and a few paper airplanes.

When I think back to that first Jesus-sharing experience, and the many I've had in the years since then, one thing always comes back to me. The greatest distance I ever had to travel for a mission trip wasn't the two-hour drive from Orange County to that orphanage in Tijuana. It wasn't the five-hour van trip from Ozark Mountain Country in Missouri to an impoverished Indian reservation in Oklahoma. It wasn't even the long, cramped, almost six-hour flight from LAX to Honolulu I once took with Jake Youmans and two dozen high school students to work among the poor on the island of Oahu. The greatest distance I ever had to travel for a mission trip – a long, perilous journey fraught with obstacles and inconvenience – was the few steps I had to take to get outside of myself.

To be honest, it's a journey I still have to take today. I'm continually taking it. I face it almost every time a new opportunity to "go and tell" presents itself. Why are those few steps so difficult? It's because mission work constitutes a radical departure from the comfortable, predictable, inwardly focused, middle-class life I'm used to. It thrusts me into a world that isn't defined by my terms. There is nothing typical about a typical mission trip; it's out of my control. Like a sheet of paper folded into a flying machine and sent soaring in whatever direction its maker decides, going into the world to engage in selfless service doesn't come with a flight plan. There are Holy Wind currents that always seem to carry me places I would never go on my own, and regardless of where I end up I always feel like I've crash-landed and made a mess of things. When I'm on a mission trip, I never fail to go to bed at the end of the day feeling used up and, yes, slightly crumpled. But here's the thing – just as I've learned that the typical mission trip is anything but typical, I've also learned that crash-landings, messes, and feeling tired and used up at the end of the day are okay. In fact, they often end up being some of the most sacred moments of a whole trip, moments where God brings glory to Himself and shows His great strength and power in the midst of great human weakness (cf. 2 Corinthians 12:9-10).

As hard as it is to get outside of myself, as difficult as those few steps are to take, and despite the fact that they haven't gotten any easier as the years have passed, I keep taking them anyway. I take those steps because I am ceaselessly amazed by what God does in me and through me when I surrender to the call of a trip. I take those steps because I always come away from a missions experience in awe of the life change I've seen in the people to whom I've ministered, and in awe of the life change I've seen in myself. I marvel at the fact that though I go to serve, I, too, am invariably served. And when I come home and report to the people who sent me all I saw God do in this place or that place, I'm overwhelmed when I see a wave of joyful eagerness sweep across the faces of men and women completely taken with the idea. It's like they're catching the dream right then and there, owning it, committing to it in their hearts. I know that when the time comes to go again, many of them will be on the team with me.

Participating in mission trips over the past 25 years has been a wonderful, faith-building experience. It has forever changed who I am and how I approach ministry. That it has never been easy or convenient is beside the point. I'm not a person who has the gifts, the driving passion, or the boundless energy to go to the ends of the earth and back countless times a year like my dear friend who has written this book. But like most Christians, I do have a driving passion and great desire to see people come to know Jesus Christ. For me, short-term missions have been a catalyst toward a long-term missional life. They can be for you too. Hop in the car, climb into the van, get on the plane, and go. It doesn't matter if you don't speak the language. You don't need any theological training. You don't really need much of anything at all – just the willingness to get outside of yourself a little bit. Short on that too? That's okay; God will take care of it. God, who has called you, is faithful, and He will do it. He will do it all.

• • • • •

Rev. Paul Stark is the president of Pillar Christian Ministries, Inc., and serves as the pastor for Zion Lutheran Church in Diggins, Missouri. He is also the Bible teacher for E-DiBS.org, a video-based, verse-by-verse study of the Scriptures delivered weekdays via e-mail. You can reach Paul and learn more about his ministry by dropping him a line at pillar_ministries@yahoo.com, or visit www.e-dibs.org to sign up for the Bible studies. They're free!

Personal Mission Perspective

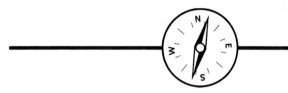

Connecting Through God
by Nick Miner

Every mission trip is unique in its own way, filled with its own distinctive experiences, people, and challenges. Mission trips challenge you to do something out of your comfort zone. Often, stepping outside of the comfort zone comes in the form of physical labor in building things, or distributing clothing and food to the cold and hungry. Other times it is simply in the relationships made with the people encountered along the way. Over the years, I have served on mission trips that have pushed me to step outside of my own comfort zone, both physically and emotionally.

During my senior year of high school, I traveled to the other side of the world to Auckland, New Zealand. This trip was different from any other mission trip I had been on before. Up to this point, the mission trips I had been on were about helping communities in need with physical work, whereas this trip was about making connections and building relationships. When I first arrived, I was expecting to dive into labor-intensive work. Instead, we read stories, sang songs, and shared the Word of God with children in the church through children's worship services. We also brought joy to many lonely elderly people who rarely had visitors. We talked, prayed, and visited with them in their homes. When I returned home from New Zealand, I felt like this trip had been more of a vacation than a mission trip. It wasn't until a few weeks after returning, when I wrote and received letters from one of the elderly women I visited, that I realized the effect this trip had on me. I learned that relationships built on mission trips are just as important as any physical labor. I realized that mission work may not always feel rewarding during the trip itself, but God still has a plan and purpose for what He wants you to accomplish. It was a great way for me to see that mission trips are not about making me feel better about myself, but instead they are about serving the purpose God has planned. Regardless of what I was doing on the trip, or who I was forming relationships with, it was always important for me to remember that the primary purpose of the mission trip is to spread the Word of God.

New Zealand may have been the farthest I have traveled for a mission trip, but I have also been on many trips in my own backyard. One of the mission trips that stands out in my mind the most was only an hour north of my hometown. This mission trip to Inglewood, in the heart of Los Angeles, California made me realize that you do not have to travel across the globe to accomplish God's work. This mission trip did involve the physical aspects I was used to, including tiling the floors, cleaning the church, and serving food to those in need. Although this trip involved more physical labor, it also gave me the chance to develop relationships with others. The difference was that instead of developing relationships with people I had never met before, I was building on the relationships I had already developed with the people who came with me on the trip. Some of my strongest friendships have been developed on mission trips because they were centered on God. On each mission trip, people are seeing you in an environment that is unfamiliar and at a time when you may be most vulnerable. But this is where the best relationships are built – and they can last a lifetime.

From Auckland, New Zealand to Inglewood, California, each mission trip I have been on has served a different purpose. It did not matter whether I was doing physical labor or singing with children – these trips have shown me that strong relationships can be built anywhere, and in any situation, as long as God is at the center. The lessons I have learned on mission trips not only apply when away from home, but in everyday life as well. Each day, you will encounter different people with different experiences that you can learn from if you take the time to listen and hear their stories. Each day of my life needs to be lived as if I am on a mission trip, because every day is a new mission from God.

> **For it is by grace you have been saved, through faith – and this is not from yourselves, it is the gift of God – not by works, so that no one can boast.**
> (Ephesians 2:8-9)

. . . . .

Nick Miner is an engineer for a general contractor. He is married to his beautiful wife, Michelle. Nick has traveled on several mission trips with Jacob Youmans, constantly building relationships and serving those in need.

Judea

Introduction to Judea

Judea is the name given to the southern kingdom of Israel. While there is a great deal of history leading up to how we got two kingdoms of Israel, the basic idea is that after King Solomon, author of the book of Proverbs and heir to King David, the kingdom was divided into two parts: the north and the south. The north kept the name Israel while the south went by the name Judea. The common name of "Jew" is actually taken from the name Judea.

The area of Judea is named after the dominant tribe of the south – Judah. The tribe derived its name from the fourth son of the patriarch Jacob (whose name God changed to Israel – Genesis 35:10) and Leah. The meaning of the name Judah is "praise and thanks." Several of the Biblical cities that you have heard of – Jerusalem, Bethany, and that little town of Bethlehem – are located within the area known as Judea. The geographical area is certainly larger than a city, and in our North American context, it could be comparable to a "state." However, the metaphorical meaning of Judea is so much more.

Metaphorically, I want us to think of Judea as people who are not Christian but are otherwise similar to us. Judeans are, for whatever reasons, not connected to Jesus Christ as Lord and Savior. Maybe they are not involved in church because no one invited them. Maybe they have prioritized worldly things over God. Maybe they are down on their luck and need a little help to get back on their feet. Maybe a tragedy or a painful past has caused them to feel separated from God. Whatever their reasons may be, God just may use you to help them see

Jesus! Judea could be across the country, or even across the
street. Let's explore how we can be missional in Judea.

What Can I Do?

In 1998, I took my Hawaiian youth group on their first mission trip. We went to Tijuana, Mexico, to the Casa de Amore orphanage where I had gone on my very first mission trip back in college. For several of the youth, it was their first time leaving the islands. For all of them, it was their first time in Mexico and their first mission trip anywhere. And for me, it was my first time being fully in charge of a mission trip! I was so excited to have them experience the joys of missions, and I was quite honored to be leading them in this adventure. This was the crucial first step in casting the vision for them of living life as a mission trip.

We had a full day of fun, VBS-type activities planned for the kids at the orphanage. My youth group students were curious about what the whole mission experience would be like, and they were excited and enthusiastic as we started the bus ride from Los Angeles Intl. Airport down to Tijuana. The drive took several hours, and crossing the border with a group of minors took a while, but we finally arrived at the orphanage.

A funny thing happened as soon as our bus pulled into the parking lot. Immediately, all of the kids in my group jumped out and got busy right away. All of the guys went with the older orphan boys across the street to play soccer in an empty dirt lot. They had old tires to mark the goals and they amazed the Hawaiian boys with their soccer skills! Half of the

Hawaiian girls went off with the older girls from the orphanage to do "girl stuff." I was not allowed in that area, as I am not a girl. But I am sure they had tons of girl fun! The other half of the Hawaiian girls took the little kids inside to play and do all sorts of "little kid stuff."

I felt very proud of my youth and the speed with which they had excitedly jumped into the mission! They all quickly found ways to serve and use their gifts. But, as I looked around the orphanage, there was one little orphan boy sitting all by himself, with a pouting frown on his face and his arms crossed. He looked too small to play with the big boys, too big to play with the little kids, and of course he wouldn't want to do any of the "girl stuff." So I went up to him to try to befriend him and show him some love.

My Spanish is very poor, but I gave it a shot anyway. I wanted to try to speak his vernacular.

"*¿Cómo te llamas?*" I said, which means, "What is your name?"

"*Victor,*" he said.

"*¿Victor?*" I replied.

"*Sí.*"

"*¡Excelente!*" I said, wondering what I could say next... Oh, I knew!

"*¿Quantos anos?*" which means, "How old are you?"

"*Cuatro,*" he said, as he held up four fingers.

"*¿Cuatro?*"

"*Sí.*"

"*¡Excelente!*" Now at this point I had completely run out of all of my conversational Spanish. But sure enough, right at that moment – right at the perfect moment – a dog ran across the parking lot. I know the Spanish word for dog. So, very excitedly I said, "Victor – look – *perro, perro!*"

"No!" he said. "Doggy!"

At that moment, one of my Hawaiian kids, Greg, came over to me. Greg was on crutches. He had multiple sclerosis, which led to lots of physical difficulties, and he had been using crutches ever since he could remember. By the grace of God, he was usually the most joy-filled kid in the group. But I could tell this was not one of those times. He crutched over to me and said, "Jake, I shouldn't have come."

"What?!" I said in disbelief. "What do you mean?" After all, we couldn't have imagined this mission trip without our buddy Greg along!

"I can't play soccer with the kids across the street. The little kids are scared of my crutches. And I'm not going to play girl games. I can't help here. I shouldn't have come."

I glanced down at sad little Victor beside me.

"Greg," I said, "you have perfect timing! Greg, meet Victor. Victor, this is Greg."

Victor smiled, and at that moment I think Victor understood more than I did! Greg smiled back and said, "Hey."

Believe it or not, Greg's Spanish was even worse than mine –
much worse! But it didn't matter one bit, because after that
little introduction, the two of them were inseparable for the
rest of the trip. Watching a Mexican orphan on the back of a
Hawaiian teen on crutches, both screaming with joy, is an
image of Jesus' love that I will never forget. They were polar
opposites, but through the love of Jesus, they were able to
connect!

· · · · ·

When we focus on our *dis*abilities instead of our abilities, we
miss out on opportunities to live life as a mission trip. While
no one can reach everyone, everyone can reach *someone*.
Now I know that may sound a bit like *Who's on First?*[5], but
the point is this: If you cannot seem to reach a particular
person, maybe God has someone else in mind to reach them.
Instead, focus on who you *can* reach.

Moses focused on his disability at first. The calling of Moses
through the burning bush is a fascinating narrative. Read
through it in Exodus chapters 3 and 4. Moses makes some of
the same excuses for not obeying and fulfilling his call that
we do today. The first excuse he makes is, **"Who am I?"**
(Exodus 3:11). He did not think he was someone special. He
certainly did not feel he was worthy of the calling. But he
soon realizes that it's *the call* that makes one worthy. It's God
who makes him special!

The next excuse Moses gave to God was essentially, "Who
are you?" (cf. Exodus 3:13). If we do not know that God is
God, then there is no way we can fulfill our calling. God
being God means that He is in control and He knows exactly
what He's doing! He doesn't call in the way the world does –
calling the richest, most talented, or best looking – but instead

He calls the ones He wants. He calls the outcast, the broken, the ones who feel the least worthy – and His power is on display through them! (cf. 2 Corinthians 12:9)

Back to Moses, we see that the excuses continue – and the next two have to do with Moses' lack of confidence in his own skill and ability. First he says, "What if no one believes me?" (cf. Exodus 4:1). He then goes on to say, **"I am slow of speech and tongue"** (Exodus 4:10). What is God's response to both of Moses' excuses about lack of ability? "I'll provide!" (cf. Exodus 4:2-9, 11-12, and 14-17). **"My power is made perfect in weakness"** (2 Corinthians 12:9). Basically, what God is saying here is this: "Focus on My calling for you, and what you can do. I'll take care of the things that you don't think you can do!" When we ask the *What if?* question from a positive perspective, we see more clearly the possibilities God has in store for us. What if we learn to trust God in the way that Moses eventually did? Lives would certainly be changed!

But Moses isn't quite there yet. At this point, he is still doubtful and insecure. And now it seems like he has completely run out of excuses. So instead of making up another one, he just comes clean and admits what he's been thinking the whole time: **"Pardon your servant, Lord. Please send someone else."** (Exodus 4:13) He didn't want to do it. He wanted God to send someone else. At least he was polite about it, but the message was clear – he didn't want to go!

God's initial response is perhaps some of the scariest words in all of Scripture: **"the LORD's anger burned against Moses"** (Exodus 4:14). The anger of God comes when we do not use the gifts, talents, and abilities we have been given. When we focus on what we think we can't do, instead of on the things we *can* do, God gets angry. Finally, Moses does as he is called – and the rest is history. By the grace of God, Moses overcomes his weaknesses and becomes arguably the greatest Israelite leader in history. He even gets to interact with Jesus at the Transfiguration (Matthew 17:3)!

The world is a big place, and sometimes we might feel so small and insignificant. To even think about changing the world can be a terrifying and overwhelming thought. But when we focus on what we *can* do with the strength God provides, we are able to live life as a mission trip. Perhaps as you've been reading through the devotions in this book, you have found yourself making excuses in your head as to why you could never actually do some of these things yourself. Maybe you are asking yourself, *But what can I do? I'm too young / too old / too shy / too inexperienced / too unqualified / too unsure of myself.* Or perhaps, like Moses, you have finally run out of excuses not to go forth and live a missional life right here at home, right in the world around you. Do not be discouraged. There is no better time than now to start focusing on what you *can* do. The world needs you!

Questions for Reflection and Discussion

1. Do you tend to focus on your abilities or your *dis*abilities? How does this viewpoint affect your ministry?

2. What excuses do you find yourself making to God as to why you can't serve Him in a particular way?

3. Write down some of these excuses and swap lists with a friend. Pray for one another in the coming weeks and ask that God will help you overcome your fears and

hesitations, and serve Him with an open mind and a willing heart.

4. We all feel small and insignificant at times. We may wonder if we can make a difference in even one person's life, let alone change the world! Make a list of some of the big and little ways you can impact someone else's life this week.

Coke Giveaway

The Coca-Cola® Company is a fascinating case study through a missional lens. The Coke® product itself was invented in 1886, and in a little over 100 years it has completely conquered the world. Coke is currently available legally in over 200 countries, and I have it on reliable account that one can get it through the black market in every single country in the world. There may be no more accurate advertising slogan than "Coke is it!" because for people around the world, Coke really *is* "it."

At the World of Coca-Cola museum in Coke's hometown of Atlanta, Georgia, one can sample over 70 different varieties of Coke from all over the world. On a recent trip to the museum with a friend, we spent about an hour trying every single one of those varieties. Some tasted very good, while others were so unpleasant that we had to spit them out! Many had a familiar taste, but some tasted like nothing we had ever tried before. The beverages at the museum are divided up by continent, so it is easy to see, from the moment you walk in, that Coke is an international global phenomenon. Coca-Cola has found a way to incorporate itself into so many different cultures by changing the taste, color, and feel of the beverage to connect with local palates – while still maintaining the look and feel of a Coke.

My personal fascination with Coke in a foreign context stems from a mission trip I took to North Africa. Our group was out riding camels through the Sahara Desert. There are still millions of nomads who have never encountered a missionary, and we were out looking for some of them. We were in the middle of nowhere. The landscape is barren but beautiful. Sand, sand, and more sand, as far as the eye can see! But out from behind a lone palm tree, a young boy, maybe seven years old and covered in desert garb, walked over to our caravan of camels. What did he want? He was interested in selling us a Coke. Without hesitation, I bought one from him. It was the best tasting Coke of my life – ice-cold in the intense heat, and sweeter than I remember Cokes being back home in the good old U.S.A.! I guess everything tastes better when you are riding on the back of a camel! I kept that Coke bottle as a souvenir, and it's sitting in my office to this day. Its curved bottle and bright red label are the same, yet the words – even the words Coca-Cola – are all in Arabic. Since that trip, I have been collecting Coke bottles from all over the world. They all look basically the same, except for the language, and yet they all tasted a little different.

While on a camping trip in the Australian bush, I got up early in the morning and went out on a prayer walk by myself. I enjoyed the peacefulness and solitude of this remote location. I saw kangaroos, birds of all shapes and sizes, beautiful vegetation, and – perhaps best of all – no sign of human beings. That is, until I saw a bright red dot on the ground up ahead. It shined brightly in the morning sunlight. As I got closer, I realized exactly what it was. It was a Coke bottle cap. I'm beginning to think there is nowhere you can go on this planet to escape Coke's presence! It seems to show up even in the most unexpected places.

We, as the Church, can learn quite a bit from Coke. The Church has been around for 2,000 years and Coke for only 100, and yet it can be argued that more people in the world have heard of Coke than Jesus. What if the Church could be found in every country and community – even in the ones where it's illegal? What if the Church was able to communicate the Gospel, in all its truth and purity, but in a way that could connect to local "palates?" St. Paul says it like this in 1 Corinthians 9:21-23 –

> **To those not having the law I became like one not having the law (though I am not free from God's law but am under Christ's law), so as to win those not having the law. To the weak I became weak, to win the weak. I have become all things to all people so that by all possible means I might save some. I do all this for the sake of the gospel, that I may share in its blessings.**

The Coca-Cola Company has found a way to "become all things to all people." Can the Church?

There is a congregation I have worked with near Austin, Texas that takes the idea of "Coke Ministry" to a whole new level. Quarterly, members of the church stand on two busy street corners in town and pass out free Cokes to the people who are driving by. The Cokes are ice-cold, completely free, and come with a business card inviting them to the church. They actually grew their church this way from the beginning, and now it's part of their DNA. Many people have joined their church over the years because they got an unexpected free Coke one Saturday afternoon!

It's interesting to watch people wrestle with accepting a free gift. In our culture, "free" usually means one of two things:

it's cheap, or there's a catch. Many people simply refuse a free Coke. Some people will not even roll down their window and acknowledge our presence. Some people try to offer us money (I actually had to turn down a $50 bill!), but we never accept money. That isn't what the day is about. It's about serving the community in a simple way. It's about a free gift – and an unexpected blessing in their day.

Many people are very appreciative. We actually got a driver of a Pepsi® truck to take a Coke one time! That was quite a sight to see! Many people ask if they can take two and give one to a friend. Of course they can! We hear lots of appreciative comments such as "Thank you!" and "How nice!" We even get a few "God bless yous." Not everyone we offer a Coke to is a non-Christian. And certainly not everyone we give a Coke to shows up for church. But it's a simple way to serve and bless the community.

One interesting thing about the Coke giveaway is that the vast majority of people we give a Coke to do not *need* a free Coke. They are driving a car with gas in it, so odds are they have the means to buy their own Coke. And yet, that congregation has grown from simply giving the free gift of an ice-cold Coca-Cola beverage. They are blessing people in a graceful and surprising way. Even if it's not something the people necessarily *need*, it's certainly something they appreciate! There is power in a thoughtful free gift!

· · · · ·

It reminds us of the story of Jesus feeding the 5,000, found in Matthew chapter 14. There are so many different elements to the story. First, there is the multiplication of the five loaves and two fish. What an incredible reminder that Jesus takes our gifts and skills, and uses them to multiply His kingdom!

Then there are the 12 baskets of leftovers. It's not a coincidence that they had 12 baskets left over, because there was one for each of His 12 doubting disciples. There is also the lesson that Jesus thanked God for the miracle even before it happened. Notice Jesus' progression in verse 19: **"Taking the five loaves and the two fish and looking up to heaven, he gave thanks and broke the loaves."** Seems like Jesus is not just praying with gratitude – but *attitude*! He has the attitude of one who trusts completely in what God can do. He is confident that His Heavenly Father will provide. He knows the Father will work a miracle, and He thanks Him before it happens! That kind of trust and understanding just might change our prayer life!

But the element of the story that is perhaps the most fascinating is that the crowd is not full of poor, destitute people. They had homes. They had means. It was just getting late, and everyone was hungry. They didn't *need* the food, and yet Jesus blessed them with a nice fish dinner anyway. The disciples wanted to send them all back to their houses, but Jesus had another idea completely. God provides for our needs even when we don't necessarily *need* it, especially in the abundance He supplies! He blesses us until our cup overflows (cf. Psalm 23:5).

To reach out to Judea – to the people who are similar to us – maybe we need to provide for their needs beyond the basic necessities. Little acts of kindness, an unexpected gift of love, and little moments of blessing could point them to a Savior who has exactly what they really need – a limitless supply of grace!

Questions for Reflection and Discussion

1. During the course of a day, count how many times you
    see or come in contact with a Coke sign or advertisement.
    Which methods of advertising do you feel are the most
    effective for this brand? What can the Church learn from
    these methods?

2. What do you think a person on the street would say about
    your church? What does this tell you about your
    congregation's strengths and weaknesses?

3. What are some ways that you can randomly bless some-
    one's day today?

Down Under

"American missionaries have had a bit of trouble over here in the past," said Rev. Bryce Clark, the Australian Lutheran pastor who served as my generous host and guide while "Down Under."

"Why is that?" I asked, rather surprised. His statement caught me off guard. I had always believed that a missionary's greatest challenge comes from having to learn the local language. Australians speak English... well, basically...

"Actually," he explained, "we have deceptively different cultures."

"Deceptively different" cultures – by this, he meant that the cultures are different, but appear similar. I had never thought about it like that before. The whole time I was visiting Australia and interacting with Australians, I was assuming we had very *similar* cultures. In fact, I was not really making a conscious effort to be as culturally sensitive as I normally strive to be when visiting "other" cultures.

I think I'm going to be processing the "deceptively different" insight for the rest of my life. At the surface level, the North American and Australian cultures are very similar. Not only is the language essentially the same, but the ideals, hopes, dreams, and lifestyles seem to be much the same. We even have a similar history of English colonization followed by revolution. With the majority of people being of Western European decent, we physically look similar. In fact, I joked that while in Australia, in contrast to recent trips to Hong Kong and El Salvador, I can actually blend in with the crowd as an over six feet tall, white male. I believe most people there think I'm Australian... until I talk – then everyone knows I'm an American... or maybe a Canadian.

Some of the differences between the United States and Australia are simple to explain, such as the fact that they have their winter months during our summer months, and vice versa. They never dream of a "white Christmas," as it's usually very hot in December. Australians also use certain terms and words that we are not accustomed to. For example, I did a few double-takes when we drove past a storefront sign that said "Chemist" – which is what they call the pharmacist. They do not have ketchup – they have squeeze bottles of tomato sauce. And tomato sauce, being blander and not as sweet, doesn't taste nearly as good on your *chips* (french fries)! When offering you a cup of coffee, they ask if you would like a "cuppa" – as in a cup of coffee. I really liked this expression and tried to bring it back to Texas with zero success.

Other differences between the two countries' cultures are a little more complex and need to be experienced. There are many subtle differences in how we interact. For example, to talk about oneself in our American culture is considered friendly and outgoing, but in Australian culture it is considered egotistical. Also, the Australian people seem to have a strong desire to blend in and follow the rules, which is in contrast to the independent American spirit that we are so proud of. One time, while we were at a restaurant, we decided we wanted to get some food for carryout even though there was a sign clearly saying "No Takeaway." I told my host that I would go turn on my American charm – and that I was sure we could get some food to go. They let me try. I smiled sweetly and tried my best to convince the restaurant staff to make an exception for us – but it didn't do any good. They adhered to the rules. Disappointed with my failure, I returned to my hosts empty-handed. They were not surprised.

The differences between our American culture and the Australian culture are subtle, yet they are there. To pretend they don't exist would be disastrous. Such a presumption has gotten many an American visitor in trouble. Instead, Pastor Clark advises it is best to observe, listen, and learn, just like you would in a completely different culture.

Maybe that's the key. We need to understand that our culture, our context, is *ours*, and every other culture falls into one of two categories: different, or deceptively different. We can even find ourselves in the deceptively different category right here in the U.S., as we travel to different parts of the country or even as we engage with local subcultures (e.g., based on age or socioeconomic status). Culture is so much more than skin color and ethnic background. Acknowledging the deeper differences allows us to realize our full potential as missionaries. If we observe, listen, and learn instead of judge and demand things be the way we are accustomed to (or want them to be), many more doors can open for ministry opportunities.

· · · · ·

St. Paul was brilliant at observing, listening, and learning when encountering a different culture. Being both a Jew and a Roman citizen, Paul encountered more than a few deceptively different cultures. In Acts chapter 17, while Paul is waiting in

Athens for Silas and Timothy to join him for their next adventure, he takes the time to walk around town. He notices all of the idols, and his heart is broken by what he observes. He feels compelled to interact with the culture and connect them to Jesus as Lord and Savior! Paul tells them in verses 22 and 23,

> **People of Athens! I see that in every way you are very religious. For as I walked around and looked carefully at your objects of worship, I even found an altar with this inscription: TO AN UNKNOWN GOD. So you are ignorant of the very thing you worship – and this is what I am going to proclaim to you.**

Notice what Paul does. There is an important progression in this cross-cultural interaction. First by saying, **"I see that in every way you are very religious,"** Paul is affirming their culture. When you affirm someone's culture, you affirm *them*. And when you affirm someone, they are more likely to be open to what you have to say. It's like the old saying, *You can catch more flies with honey than with vinegar.* St. Paul does not agree with their culture – yet he still is able to affirm it and affirm the people.

Second, when Paul says **"I walked around and looked carefully at your objects of worship,"** it shows that he has done his homework. He has observed. He has listened. He has learned. Notice that he didn't just walk around. He walked around and looked *carefully*. He observed and studied their ways, and his studying guided his interaction with their culture.

Finally, Paul says, **"I even found an altar with this inscription: TO AN UNKNOWN GOD. So you are ignorant of**

the very thing you worship – and this is what I am going to proclaim to you." After he affirms the culture and shows that he has studied it carefully, he then connects the culture to Jesus (as more fully described in verses 24-34). But here is the interesting thing. If Paul had started there, no one would have listened to him. But with this progression of interaction, people of a different culture connected to Jesus.

I had an incredible time interacting with and learning about the deceptively different culture of Australia. I also had fun encountering the variety of unique animals found only on the Australian continent. I got to observe many kangaroos, especially the scary ones that hopped in front of our car! (As payback, I ate kangaroo steaks on several occasions!) I was fortunate to see a very rare wombat in the wild. I also saw a few emus, although they were in captivity.

At one point during my stay, while admiring the coat of arms of Australia, I noticed it includes a kangaroo and an emu. "Guess why we have the roo and the emu on our coat of arms?" asked Pastor Clark.

"Because they are native and unique to Australia," I answered, believing I had observed, listened, and learned about this deceptively different culture.

"Well if that were the case," Pastor Clark said, "we could have put any number of animals on there. We chose the kangaroo and the emu because they physically cannot go backward. They aren't built that way. They can only go forward, and that's our hope for Australia – that we will only go forward."

I like that! And as we observe, listen, and learn about what it means to be missional and live life as a mission trip, it is my prayer that we only go forward in our understanding of others and how best to connect them to Jesus. By the grace of God, may we only go forward.

Questions for Reflection and Discussion

1. How do you respond when you encounter cultures that are different from your own? Do you take the time to observe, study, and understand, or do you tend to make quick evaluations and judgments?

2. Do you feel like you are mostly moving forward or backward in your life? Why?

3. What are some ways you can become more observant of those around you?

The Gun

One of the more interesting missional challenges of my ministry was when I was asked to run a weekend-long youth gathering of about a thousand participants – youth and youth leaders – in Palm Springs, California. Our planning team really didn't want to have a typical gathering, with a speaker as the main event, a band, and a dance. We wanted the participants to experience life as a mission trip. We knew that many of these kids had never been on a mission trip before, and so we brainstormed ways to give them the opportunity to work together to serve others. We wanted to give them a missional experience in just a few hours.

So the focal point of the gathering was a massive citywide cleanup in one of the rougher neighborhoods of Palm Springs. This was not an easy undertaking, by any stretch of the imagination. We had to find enough meaningful work to occupy close to a thousand teenagers for several hours. We got connected with the city council, and upon completion of the event we actually got a community service award from them! We had groups picking up trash, painting, cleaning up the property of some residents, and doing odd jobs for folks in the community. Interestingly enough, however, we had to deal with more than a few youth leaders who did not like the idea of spending time during the weekend "out serving." They were looking for more entertaining activities – not this. We received plenty of complaints and lots of questions, but every group participated. Change is tough, and not everyone will embrace change – especially at first.

The event went very well. Everyone worked hard, and the students (and even some of their leaders) caught the vision! We had NBC and CBS news crews there to film and interact with our students. Del Taco was generous enough to donate lunch for everyone, and they even brought their spokesperson, Del Taco Dan (Gregg Binkley)! To Southern California teenagers in the early 2000s, there was no bigger local celebrity than Del Taco Dan. He was gracious enough to give out autographs and take photos with them. Most of all, I was so proud of how wonderfully the kids and their youth leaders served the community that day. For many of these students and adults, it was their first time doing something like this. Mission work is not a part of every youth ministry, let alone one of the most important parts, as it was in ours. We had tried very hard to have this gathering model our core values, and I think we succeeded.

When you clean up a neighborhood, it's very messy work. There was literally trash everywhere. We ended up finding all sorts of things which I won't describe. But I do want to mention what one of the groups found that day – a loaded gun. Two of the teenage boys found it and immediately took it to their youth leader. He assumed it wasn't real, so he had his group pose and take pictures James Bond-style or Charlie's Angels-style with all of the kids in his youth group. Thinking about this story now, more than ten years later, still freaks me out! Someone could have been seriously injured or killed! We have to be so careful with those God has put in our flock. I truly believe it is by the mercy and grace of God that no one was seriously hurt that day.

Thank God that one of the college volunteers happened to see all this from afar. He walked over to the group as they were taking pictures, and calmly asked for the gun. They gave it to him without question, and then he quickly unloaded it. As the realization of what they had been playing with set in, the group was shocked and shaken. Suddenly we had a group of teens with a lot of questions. The college volunteer brought the gun to me, and we immediately called the police. A squad car arrived within minutes – which shows you the severity of the situation! The officers were incredibly thankful that no one was hurt. They asked to meet the students who found the gun, so we brought over the two teenage boys. The cops shook both of their hands, and thanked them again and again. With tears welling up in his eyes, one of the police officers said, "Gentlemen, you saved a life today by finding this. You most likely saved a police officer's life, as many of the guns on the street are used to target the police. Who knows, you may have saved *my* life! Thank you!"

I have never seen two teenage boys with bigger smiles. Ear to ear is an understatement. They were soaking in every word from the police officer. Considering that many encounters involving teenagers and police are often due to negative circumstances, this was an example where both parties were very respectful and excited to be working together. The two young men had not realized that they might have saved a life – they were just picking up trash! But when they understood the significance of what they had done, and the importance of their service to the community, they couldn't wait to get back and clean up some more!

· · · · ·

Do you think it's possible to save a life and not even realize it? It seems like a pretty major thing to do for someone! – and yet I think it happens all the time when we live life as a mission trip. We will most likely never know how our words and actions may affect the people we encounter. The kindness we show to a random stranger just might be the thing that helps lead them to God. The invitation we give to a friend to come to church with us just might be the thing that connects them to Jesus. All of the seemingly simple gestures of kindness we do – and even the not-so-glamorous, picking-up-trash kinds of things – can be used by God to save lives!

Think about the Samaritan woman at the well in John chapter 4. She was just going about her day as usual. This woman came to draw water, as everyone needed to do, and in the midst of her normal routine she encounters Jesus. Note that she didn't meet Him at the temple or at a place where important people or scholars hang out – she encountered Him at the town well. Read their interaction in John 4:1-42. Through the course of their conversation, Jesus tells the woman who He is – the Messiah – the promised one (verse 26). Immediately after that, **"leaving her water jar, the woman went back to the town and said to the people, 'Come, see a man who told me everything I ever did. Could this be the Messiah?' They came out of the town and made their way toward him."** (verses 28-30)

She left her water jar! Her whole purpose of being there was quickly forgotten and left behind when she encountered Jesus. And what did she do next? She went back and told everyone what she had learned. She was on a mission to share Jesus with others! It became her highest priority. And the people came. They wanted to see for themselves!

When the townspeople came to encounter Jesus themselves, their lives too were saved. In verse 42 they say: **"We no longer believe just because of what you said; now we have**

heard for ourselves, and we know that this man really is the Savior of the world." Living life as a mission trip is not only about sharing the good news of Jesus with other people – it's also about inviting people to come and see, hear, and experience Him for themselves. Jesus will do all the work. But your call is to invite people to come see!

Questions for Reflection and Discussion

1. Do you think you have ever saved a life? If so, in what way?

2. Is there anyone you could credit for saving your life?

3. What are some ways in which you can invite people to "come and see?" Who can you invite?

Top Ten Excuses for Why I Can't Go on a Mission Trip

"It Costs Too Much Money"

I often wonder what God thinks when we blame finances. I think some people actually believe that God could have a money shortage. But, please rest assured – God has plenty of money! He created the whole world, after all. He has all the resources He needs!

While we should always try to be good stewards of all that God has given us, we are also told in Matthew chapter 6 not to worry about resources, including money. Here is an excerpt from what Jesus says there:

> **So do not worry, saying, 'What shall we eat?' or 'What shall we drink?' or 'What shall we wear?' For the pagans run after all these things, and your heavenly Father knows that you need them. But seek first his kingdom and his righteousness, and all these things will be given to you as well. (verses 31-33)**

Did you catch that last part? Seek His kingdom and all these things will be given to you. That's what a mission trip is! It's seeking God's kingdom and showing others the kingdom.

There is a God economy, and when we trust – He will provide!

One way that God can provide is through fund-raising activities. So, the next time someone tells you they can't go on a mission trip because it costs too much money, do what I've done many times – hand them a sponge and a bucket of soapy water. My experience is that parishioners and well-wishing townspeople are suddenly very interested in the cleanliness of their car when they know the funding of a mission trip is on the line!

#7

"I'm Not a Strong Enough Christian"

I've actually heard this one quite a bit over the years. This excuse means different things to different people. Some people love to blame their lack of Bible knowledge, but often their worry is less tangible than that. What does "strong enough" even mean? Is there a measuring stick on which we must reach a certain level to be effective on a mission trip? Is it like the "you must be this tall to ride" sign at the entrance of a roller coaster at Disneyland? If you don't measure up, you can't go on the ride of a lifetime?

Jesus says, **"if you have faith as small as a mustard seed, you can say to this mountain, 'Move from here to there,' and it will move. Nothing will be impossible for you."** (Matthew 17:20) Even the smallest amounts of faith enable you to do miraculous things for Jesus! And if you're still thinking that you're not a strong enough Christian, don't forget that it's not about you – it's about Jesus working in you and through you! One of the most important things for you to remember when it comes to living life as a mission trip is that Jesus will do all the work – you just have to go!

Personal Mission Perspective

A New Zealand Mission Trip
by Dave Talmage

I have had the pleasure of accompanying Jake Youmans on numerous mission trips around the world. To me, the most memorable trip was our time in Auckland, New Zealand. We took 24 high school students on a 10-day trip where we had the opportunity to minister to students and adults from a sister Missouri Synod congregation.

Our responsibilities while in New Zealand were to establish and lead a weeklong Vacation Bible School program for the youth of the church and the surrounding community. To put students together from two different cultures can be a bit daunting, and it takes time for everyone to acclimate. But put a basketball in their hands, and they come together quickly.

Each day started off with a small worship service where breaking the ice with silly songs became a pleasure instead of routine. The more student involvement, the easier it was to integrate our two cultures.

On one of our days in Auckland, we had the privilege of serving in a Lutheran retirement community. It was a cold and rainy day, but with smiles and willing hearts, we washed windows, pulled weeds, cleaned siding, or helped with whatever our hosts needed. The best part of the day was the time spent inside with our hosts, talking about life, church, and Jesus over homemade scones and coffee. What a great way to witness to others.

Another night was spent assisting the members of the congregation in feeding the homeless. This is a ministry that is done weekly at the church for the community of Auckland. We met some of the most gracious and thankful people that were happy to have young adults to talk to and listen to.

As I mentioned earlier, this was one of my favorite trips. I enjoyed getting to know the children and spending time in the community. I feel that we were able to make a difference in their lives.

· · · · ·

Dave Talmage has been involved in youth ministry at St Paul's Lutheran Church in Orange, California for the past 15 years. In that time, he has been privileged to travel the world with Jake Youmans on many mission trip adventures. Currently Dave is a Grocery Category Manager for Unified Grocers.

Samaria

Introduction to Samaria

In the New Testament, it seems like the only people worse than Gentiles are Samaritans! The Jews viewed them as "half-breeds," as their ancestors were both Assyrian and Hebrew. Jews did not associate with Samaritans. But surprise, surprise – Jesus changed everything! He not only talked to Samaritans, but even to Samaritan women (John 4:1-26)! He healed Samaritans (Luke 17:11-19)! He even made a Samaritan the good guy in one of His parables (Luke 10:25-37)! Geographically, Samaria is between Galilee, where Jesus was raised and where many of His disciples were from, and Judea, where He did much of His ministry.

Metaphorically, Samaria represents people who are in many ways not like us. The differences may be ethnic, economic, or lifestyle. "Samaritans" generally would not feel comfortable in our church. People tend to go to worship with others similar to them. But Jesus has called us to be His witnesses in Samaria as well. If we only witness to people we are comfortable with, we are not being responsive to the complete message of Jesus! Samaria could be one of your greatest challenges yet!

A Note about the Apache Mission Stories

In the Samaria section, you are going to read several stories about our adventures on the White Mountain Apache Reservation in Arizona. There are stories of other "Samarias" as well, but I think this particular place may need a little more explanation before you dive into this section. My first trip to Apache was in 2001, and since that time I have visited the tribe from one to four times a year, every single year. There has not been a time interval of more than twelve months since that very first Apache trip the fall of 2001.

In my life, this tribe has been an incredible, life-changing "Samaria" experience. I have spent more nights sleeping on the Apache land than anywhere except my own home. The Reservation has changed the lives of the hundreds of students I have led there over the years. This place is one of the things my brother Nathan credits with saving his life. Apache has motivated me and inspired my missional thinking in ways I am still processing, and I have a very special bond with this place.

The history of Native Americans, and the Apache in particular, is not a pleasant one. I believe most of you know the basics. The more I learn, the more it angers me. One of my favorite shirts has a group of Apache Warriors on it and the caption says, "Apache Homeland Security – Fighting Terrorists since 1492." The word "apache" in the Apache language actually means "enemy." For 500 years, their story has been one of brutality, broken promises, and oppression.

Visiting the reservation has often not been easy. We have had to take several students to the hospital for a variety of ailments. Every trip, someone ends up with pretty serious flu-like symptoms, and on one trip, 16 of the 21 participants got violently ill. On our first few trips, kids would throw rocks at us and tell us to "Go home!" The kids would steal anything that wasn't bolted down. We've lost hundreds of dollars to theft. We've had windows on our vehicles smashed. We've had people bang on the doors of the building we're staying in at 4:00 A.M. – just to freak us out. We've stayed in rooms with no heat in the freezing dead of winter, and no air circulation in the scorching heat of summer. We have been told "White men cannot be trusted." We have been marginalized due to the color of our skin. But we have also made lifelong friends, and we have seen people come to Jesus in the process.

Through it all, we have tried to continue to love like Jesus would love. We have tried to focus on our similarities as human beings – not on our differences. We have tried to show those who still worship the sun the power in worshiping the One who created the sun. And while we have failed many, many times, we have also seen God work in miraculous ways many, many times!

I truly believe this book would not be possible without the White Mountain Apache relationships God has blessed us with. I have had a dream since 2004 that we would be able to place a full-time missionary with the tribe. There were many people over the years who I thought would be that person. Matt Wingert spent a summer there by himself. Several others spent weeks here and there. And by the grace of God, in August 2012 that dream became a reality as Lydia Humphries started her yearlong internship on the White Mountain Apache Reservation! And as she finished that up, she told me in April of 2013 that she will continue to be serving in Apache for the foreseeable future! Our journeys to the reservation are a reminder that we need to be patient and just let God work! Everything will work out in His good and perfect time!

The Miracle

One of my favorite things about going to Apache is our lack of agenda. We want to serve however we can. All we really know for certain is the day we're arriving and the day we're leaving – and sometimes even those days can change! We never know what we will end up doing while we are there, or how God will use us. It's always an adventure! Sadly, I have seen so many well-meaning youth ministry folks come to the reservation with their preprogrammed agenda of how they will serve the Apache people – and inevitably one of two things happens. Either they get frustrated and never come back, or they quickly realize that they need to throw their agenda out the window and just dive in! Apache is a fantastic place to learn flexibility! (Or, it can be a very frustrating place to learn flexibility, depending on your perspective.)

In all the years we've been serving at Apache, we have done many different kinds of things to help out. There was the time we chopped wood for days on end because one of the little old ladies in the village didn't have any firewood and winter was coming. We were determined to get the job done for her, but inevitably we were not doing it quite right – so this eighty-year-old Apache woman picked up an axe and showed us how to *really* chop wood! She was quicker, stronger, and more efficient than most of the guys on our team! Over the years, we have painted countless buildings on the reservation – and I honestly believe that some of these buildings were held together by that paint! We have torn down fences and mended fences – both literally and metaphorically! We have sat in people's homes and listened to their stories for hours and hours. We have played tag and chase, and even tagged a few kids who were not playing... yet! One time, we refereed the youth basketball leagues for eight hours straight. We had two refs, but only one whistle. That was a fun challenge! But throughout our days of faith-filled service and hard work, we have consistently found that being flexible opens more doors for sharing Jesus than going in with a fixed agenda of our own. Each person out there has very different needs. By serving people wherever they really need help, God's love and concern for them is demonstrated all the more powerfully.

I especially enjoy the times when we all pile into the van, head off into a neighborhood, pull over somewhere, and then pray together for God's direction. This always leads us to knock on a random house, where we ask the person or family living there how we can be of service to them. Of course, this means we must be very open-minded and ready for just about anything. This method of serving might be uncomfortable for some people, but I thrive on it. You never know what's going to happen! And for me, the fact that it's unpredictable makes it so much fun!

During one such experience, after sitting in the van and praying for God's guidance, we knocked on a home that looked to be in pretty bad shape. An elderly Apache woman named Carla opened the door and asked if she could help us.

"Actually," I said, "we wanted to know if there is anything we can do to help *you*!"

"Well," she said, pausing and turning to look inside at her family gathered around the kitchen table, "nothing works in my house. Come on in, if you want."

Now, let me just state that when she said "nothing works," she wasn't kidding! The electricity didn't work. The water didn't work. The propane gas canister was empty. The roof leaked. For the first time in my life, I was beginning to think that the word "nothing" was actually an understatement! I looked at my ragtag band of Jesus-loving high school students, and I told Carla that we would do our best to help her however we could. But deep down, I honestly doubted whether we could do much to make a dent in the situation.

We started by sending a few students up into the attic and a few students under the house to look for disconnects with the plumbing and electrical wiring. As they went off to these locations, they turned and asked me, "What exactly are we looking for?"

"When you see it, you'll know it!" I assured them, even though I had no idea either. But that was a good enough response for them!

After several trips to Home Depot® and several days of hard labor, we started to see some progress with the house. We found the electrical disconnect in the attic, and with a few pieces of new wire and a lot of electrical tape, we were able to get the power running to the house again. After a little bit of digging in the backyard, we discovered where the water pipes were broken, and with some new pipe we repaired those issues as well. Another group of students were up on the roof of the house, patching the holes that led to the leaks. They almost got as much roofing tar on the roof as they did on themselves! But within a few days, the roof was sealed and as good as new.

One of the college students, Ryan, was put in charge of building a bathroom sink cabinet out of the scrap wood that was lying around outside in the yard. He looked very professional as he carefully measured the pieces, sawed them, and hammered everything together. The finished product actually looked like a bathroom cabinet! I was really impressed, and at one point I asked him, "Have you ever built anything like this before?"

"Only with LEGO®s!" he replied.

All in all, the place was starting to look pretty good! But we noticed that it was hard for us to connect with the family and engage them in conversation. Carla was a very quiet woman who did not say much, and her family would come and go but they spoke even less to us. I asked her son if he would like to help us, but he politely refused. Several of the students asked me if they even appreciated all of our work, but I explained to them some of the cultural differences, and reminded them that we are doing this for God and not for men.

After three days of very hard work, Carla pulled me aside, and in a very matter-of-fact way she said, "Jake, you all are my miracle."

"What do you mean?" I asked.

"The other day," she said, "I was talking to my son and daughter. My son is unemployed and an alcoholic – and he was threatening to kill himself. My daughter just got out of jail and is pregnant. The father of her baby is still in jail. My son and daughter were saying how hopeless and worthless life is. But I told them, 'No! God will provide a miracle for us.' And at that moment you knocked on my door. *You're* my miracle."

I was speechless. I had never been called a miracle before, and to be honest I didn't feel very miraculous. I felt tired, sweaty, and dirty, or shall I say – normal. But maybe that's the whole point. God can use a bunch of dirty, sweaty servants to do incredible things through such humble things as a patched roof, a functional bathroom, and a working stove. God can work miracles, even when the circumstances don't *feel* miraculous.

· · · · ·

In Acts chapter 3, we see Peter and John at the Temple where they encounter a disabled man begging for money. They do not have any, because being a full-time disciple was certainly not lucrative. But they also knew that this man needed something more powerful and lasting than a few coins to pay for his next meal. He needed to connect with Jesus. So Peter said to the man, **"Silver or gold I do not have, but what I do have, I give you. In the name of Jesus Christ of Nazareth, walk."** (verse 6) And he did! He got up and walked. He had asked for money, but received a miracle instead.

God is still working miracles! Perhaps there is nothing more miraculous than living the missional life, day in and day out, whether we are halfway across the globe or right in our own backyard. It isn't a mind-set that we only pull out when we are away from home on a mission trip. Instead, it is who we are, every day of our lives. It can be seen in the way that we approach everyone we meet with a sincere desire to serve them, wherever they have the greatest need. By living out this "miracle," the miracle then spreads. The love of Jesus connects with even the most hopeless among us, and gives them His hope.

Every person we meet has a story. And in His divine purpose and plan, God can connect those stories and work miracles. The beggar had begged for years, and had only gotten a handful of spare change in return. Carla had countless conversations with her children about looking to Jesus as their hope, even when things looked hopeless. In both circumstances, it didn't seem like things would ever change for the better. But something was different that day, because God connected them with a miracle. And that's the amazing thing about God. You never know when or how He is going to work His miracles! But what an honor it is when He chooses to use you!

Questions for Reflection and Discussion

1. What miracles have you seen God perform in your life?

2. Do you feel like you have ever been a miracle in someone else's life? Explain.

3. What changes could you make in your own "preplanned agenda" in order to be more flexible and open to serving others wherever they have a need?

Toilets

Is there anything more practical and necessary, while at the same time absolutely disgusting, as a toilet? I don't feel the need to go into great detail as to why this is so, but I want to simply ask: Have you ever been somewhere when you needed a toilet and did not have one? Especially in our American context, this is a major dilemma. I know that I certainly take the toilet for granted more times than not!

When you travel the world, you soon realize that not every country and culture values a good clean latrine as much as ours does. Many areas do not have plumbing that allows for toilet paper to be flushed away, so a special trash can next to the toilet is required. In some regions, the locals simply put a hole in the ground and call it a toilet – even at restaurants and other public venues. It's always fun to take people on mission trips and have them experience this kind of "rest room" for the very first time! Many young ladies have impressed me with their pure resourcefulness and lack of fear in these foreign contexts. The phrase "when in Rome" certainly rings true when it comes to bathroom facilities.

Our times in Apache have always been guided by one key philosophy. We will do *anything* to help out and to bring the love of Jesus into people's lives. No job is too big or too small. No job is too weird or too far out of our comfort zone.

We are certainly not skilled in everything, but we will try our best to help with anything we can!

In addition, before we leave on our trip, we ask around in our home community if anyone has access to any supplies or resources that could be of particular use on the reservation. God has blessed us with so many amazing donations over the years – everything from toys, clothes, and playground equipment to paint and other construction materials. Nothing goes to waste. God has provided all sorts of ways and means to use everything given to us. One year, our request for materials was answered by a manager of a plumbing supply company, who offered us twelve brand new toilets with all the fixings!

We happily accepted the toilets, and received a crash course on how to properly install them (it's really not as complicated as you might think... but it's messy!). Then we rented a trailer, and hauled them out to the reservation to bless twelve families with a brand new toilet! It was rather amusing to see the look on people's faces when we knocked on random houses and asked if they needed a new toilet installed. Most people said no – but all were extremely grateful for such a practical offer. Nevertheless, as you can imagine, it did not take long to find good homes for those twelve brand new toilets.

The new toilets were greatly appreciated by their new owners. Many of the old toilets we removed hadn't worked properly for years! When there is no money to call a plumber – if there even is a qualified plumber nearby to call – people simply have to make do with what they have. It was inspiring for us to see how much these new toilets meant to people. Think about how often you take for granted something as basic and necessary as a toilet.

Now, let me just add that finding homes for the toilets – and actually installing them – are two very different things. The intermediate step (removing the old toilet) is a doozy. I do not need to go into detail as to what is usually all over the old toilet, as well as on the floor and walls around it. It's a humbling experience to take out an old, dirty toilet. It's also important to be sure the area where the new toilet fits into the floor is clean, so a proper seal is created. It was not a pretty job, but I was so proud of my students who were willing to serve others in this way. This particular Apache trip would have made a fantastic episode of the television show *Dirty Jobs*! In fact, we did not even have a shower to clean up in after we were done. But, when each new toilet was installed and working properly, it was truly a thing of beauty!

While lying on a floor covered in human bodily fluids and excrement, fiddling with a toilet bowl covered in more of the same, I couldn't help but think of Jesus' words, **"whatever you did for one of the least of these brothers and sisters of mine, you did for me"** (Matthew 25:40). We did it for Jesus. It was dirty, smelly, and absolutely so gross that if we had stopped to think about it, we would have lost our lunches! But we did it for Jesus!

$$\cdots\cdots$$

Jesus tells a story about judgment day at the end of Matthew chapter 25. In it, He uses the metaphor of "sheep" and "goats." The sheep are those who believe in Jesus as Lord and Savior, and the goats do not. All of the nations of the world are there, and everyone is put into one of these two categories. You are either a sheep or a goat – there is no gray area. The sheep then are ushered into heaven, while the goats are banished to hell.

One aspect of the story of The Sheep and the Goats **(Matthew 25:31-46)** that I find compelling is that the people have no idea (verses 39 and 44) that they – the sheep – did it (or they – the goats – did not do it) for Him. The sheep just did what came naturally to them (i.e., follow) and the goats did what was natural to them as well (i.e., *not* follow). The sheep responded, not even knowing that it was for Jesus. Sheep do sheep things, and goats do goat things.

That's what it's like to live life as a mission trip! It's all about living a life so kind, compassionate, and loving that it just becomes an extension of who we are. We don't have to stop and think – we just act. We *respond*. And with that type of kindness and compassion, there is no job too big or too small or even too disgusting. All of it – even the filthy, excrement-laden "stuff" – is done for Jesus!

Questions for Reflection and Discussion

1. What is the most disgusting thing you have ever done for Jesus? Why did you do it?

2. Have you ever done something and not realized that it was actually for Jesus until later on? How did that happen?

3. What are some ways in which you have encountered the "least of these?"

Airplane Seatmates

I will admit to you up front that I can be the annoying, talkative guy sitting next to you on the airplane. You never know how God's going to use those conversations! Your seatmate could be a divinely inspired appointment. Plus, I'm a huge fan of the TV show *Lost*, which means I know that at any minute the plane could crash on a deserted island, and to survive I will need the help and assistance of my seatmates. If alliances break out, I want to be sure I have people on my side! But seriously, by talking to the person sitting next to me on the airplane, I believe we are starting to form a potential future alliance.

On one particular airplane ride, I sat down right next to two gentlemen holding hands. It was obvious to me from the beginning that our belief systems were a little different, but I did not let that hinder my "befriending airplane seatmate" ritual. I introduced myself to these two gentlemen, and away the conversation went. We were all flying from Honolulu to San Francisco, so we talked about the highlights of their trip. They had the greatest vacation of their lives together in Hawaii. It was the first time for both of them. We talked about Hawaiian music and hula. We talked about our home towns. They expressed a desire to move to Hawaii permanently someday, and they were very jealous that I got to live there!

Then they asked, "What do you do for a living, Jake?"

"I'm in Youth Ministry," I said.

Their chins hit the ground. The conversation came to an abrupt halt. They somehow then synchronized the turning of their heads to avoid looking at me, and physically scooted over a few inches to avoid touching me. I was being judged because of my vocation! I found it fascinating that they were judging me at this point, because I knew their beliefs and mine were different from the very beginning – yet I didn't shun or judge. They didn't hide anything and I didn't either. I had tried to befriend them and show love to them – yet when they found out about my beliefs from my occupation, they instantly judged me.

· · · · ·

These word of Jesus are recorded in Mark 13:13 as well as in Luke 21:17 – **"Everyone will hate you because of me."** Rather blunt, isn't it? Really – everyone? "Hate" seems like such a strong word. Why does the world hate us? The verse is pretty clear: because of Jesus. Jesus reminds us in John 15:18 that the world hated Him first. Ironically, they hated Him because He is perfect. Our sinful and imperfect nature hates anything that is perfect because we ourselves cannot achieve it. His perfection is impossible for us to comprehend.

My mother always warned me as a kid that when you hate someone, it means you wish they were dead! The people, in their jealousy and resentment, wished Jesus was dead. He allowed the world to hate Him, which they did – even to the point of judging Him falsely and eventually crucifying Him. Jesus endured all of this, for you and for me.

In the book of Acts, we see how the followers of Jesus were hated as well. Stephen, who was not one of the original twelve disciples, was the first to endure the full brunt of this hatred. In Acts 6-7, as he preached the good news of Jesus, people became so angry that they dragged him out of the city and stoned him. He was the first of many, many followers of Jesus to lose their lives for His sake.

So if everyone hates us because we belong to Jesus, how are we to respond? Should we hate them back? An eye for an eye and a tooth for a tooth (cf. Leviticus 24:19-20) – that would make logical sense, right? But in Matthew 5:44, Jesus says, **"love your enemies and pray for those who persecute you."** *Love* is our response. People in our "Samaria" are accustomed to being judged. They feel hated. They feel like there are enemies at every turn. But our calling is to love them and pray for them.

Right after my seatmates turned away from me, I started praying – and then I kept talking to them and did my best to be kind, friendly, funny, and conversational. And a wonderful thing happened. Within a few minutes, things were back to normal. When they realized I wasn't going to judge them, we interacted, joked, and talked for the remainder of the flight. We never talked about Jesus specifically, but I believe I let my actions do the talking. Love really is a universal language.

It is so easy for us to judge others! The way someone looks, the way someone dresses, the way someone talks, the way someone acts – in fact, everything about a person – can be an opportunity for us to make assumptions about them and find fault. When we sit in judgment, what we are really doing is focusing on our differences. But what would happen if, when we met someone new, we made a point of focusing on the *similarities* – the common ground that we both share?

Looking for similarities can be challenging at times, but that also makes it fun! When you discover things you both have in common, it can lead to deeper conversations – and those conversations just might lead to Jesus! Or as St. Peter says in 1 Peter 3:15-16,

> **Always be prepared to give an answer to everyone who asks you to give the reason for the hope that you have. But do this with gentleness and respect, keeping a clear conscience, so that those who speak maliciously against your good behavior in Christ may be ashamed of their slander.**

Considering all of the "open mouth and insert foot" moments during Peter's ministry that are recounted in Scripture, his wisdom comes from lots of experience!

As we are missional in Samaria, we have to be prepared to be hated and judged by others. We have to be ready for the resentment and hurt feelings of generations past to express themselves. But the command does not change. Our call is to love and pray. And we pray that in our loving, they may see Jesus – the author of love!

Questions for Reflection and Discussion

1. Think of a person whom you have found very difficult to love. Why is it so hard to love them? What are some ways you can reach out to them and show them love?

2. Have you felt hated by the world because you belong to Jesus? Why or why not?

3. How can you focus on similarities verses differences when you meet someone new?

Stay in the Van

For me, one of the best things about serving in youth ministry is getting to drive the youth group van! I have driven vans just about everywhere – from up to the top of an active volcano in Hawaii, to across New Zealand's North Island (on the "wrong" side of the road, mind you!). I imagine that if you added up all the miles I have logged driving vans over the years, I could have been to the moon by now. Interestingly enough, my parents owned a big red and white van back when I was a teenager, so I can honestly say that I've been driving vans since I first learned how to drive!

Only the *captain* can drive the van. It's a position of power and leadership. When driving a car, someone might think of it as "sitting in the driver's seat," but no one dares to dream of sitting in the pilot's seat of a van. It's a position of respect and authority. In fact, one of the biggest differences between our youth mission trips and adult mission trips is that the adults think they can drive my van! But the youth know better!

I have driven a van all over the White Mountain Apache Reservation. I have transported droves of kids for various ministry programs. When we are out doing ministry around the reservation, our usual routine goes something like this: I pull the van into a driveway, order a few students to get out, lead them to the front door of the home, knock on the door, ask if/how we can help, offer to pray for them, listen to their stories, etc. I was the leader of the group, and I took charge of everything. After all, I drove the van!

I had been doing this for years and with hundreds of students in the back of the van. But then it finally happened. It was a rather normal day on a rather normal trip to Apache with a rather normal group of students – and yet it happened. I pulled up to a house, and the students whose names I called hopped out ready to start their mission. But instead of waiting for my direction, they came over to my driver's side window and told me, "Stay in the van. We don't need you. We got this!"

What?! You guys got this? You don't need me? You're just a bunch of teenagers! I'm the youth minister! I'm the captain, the leader... I drive the van!

Now, please understand that I didn't actually say any of this. I was actually so caught off guard that I didn't say anything at all. I just nodded, and off they went!

I sat and watched them as they headed into the house. I watched them interact with the people, and I watched them eventually pray and lay hands on the people. And then it hit me. *This is what I have been preparing them for. This is what I have been training them for. This is exactly what I have wanted all along – for them to take their faith adventure seriously and embrace it as their own!* This has been the fruit of much work – my own, and that of many other loving adult volunteer counselors. Like a proud coach watching his team claim a huge victory, I just sat back in my seat and smiled.

. . . . .

Proverbs 22:6 says, **"Start children off on the way they should go, and even when they are old they will not turn from it."** While this verse is often applied to parenting, I want to suggest an even broader application. All Christians have the responsibility to model the missional life. Think about how many people it took to nudge *you* in the right direction. I know that countless people have given their time and energy to guide me along in God's path to make me who I am today. We can impact lives and empower others when we model the way to go. And eventually, we can be told to "stay in the van." Jesus' way of paraphrasing this is: **"Well done, good and faithful servant!"** (Matthew 25:21)

Two of the biggest compliments I have ever received in ministry came during my first Apache trip with college students from Concordia University Texas. Besides having Texas college students on the reservation for the very first time, I also invited out some "old pros" – some of my former youth group students from St. Paul's Lutheran Church in Orange, California, who had served with me in Apache over the years. It was a fun "clash of cultures," where my two worlds collided as half the crowd knew me as "Dr. Youmans" and half the crowd knew me as "Uncle Jake."

The groups got along wonderfully and worked very well together, all the while sharing the stereotypes they each had of Texans and Californians. At one point, while painting a house, a Concordia Texas student and a former youth group student struck up a conversation. Eventually, the college student asked the other, "Are you *sure* you never took any of Dr. Youmans's classes? You talk just like him."

Laughing, he answered, "No. I just *lived* it for eight years!"

What a humbling and profound response. What a great reminder that we teach with our life. We model what it means to be a follower of Jesus, and how to be missional in everything we do. And this young man had gotten it; he had learned the lesson. By the way, this former youth group student who said that he "lived it" for eight years is also the same student, Matt Wingert, who told me to stay in the van several years before! The student had become the teacher. The student was teaching and modeling what he had been taught and modeled.

On that very same trip, during our final night on the Apache reservation, our group came together for a closing affirmation and processing time. One of my Concordia Texas students, who was accustomed to seeing me in a classroom setting, kindly affirmed me by saying, "Dr. Youmans, it was so much fun to see you out of your element."

Upon hearing that comment, all of my former youth group students burst out in laughter. Seeing the confused and somewhat hurt look on the Texas student's face, one of the former youth group students politely responded, "Sorry, but you just don't understand. People back at our home, even those who barely know us, would laugh at that comment too – because *this* is what we do. *This is* our element!"

This is who we are – missionaries. This is what we do – anything! – in order to spread the love and grace of Jesus. Our "element" is anywhere people need Jesus – which just happens to be *everywhere!* By the way, the Concordia Texas student who said it was fun to see me out of my element is Lydia Humphries, who is now a full-time missionary on the Apache reservation. She is completely in her element now on the White Mountain Apache Reservation, modeling and

nudging others in "the way!" I love it when the student becomes the teacher!

Questions for Reflection and Discussion

1. What do you think is your "element?"

2. What kinds of circumstances challenge you to break out
   of your "element?"

3. Is there someone in your life who needs to hear the words,
   "Well done, good and faithful servant!" (Matthew
   25:21)? Is there a teacher or special influence in your life
   that you need to thank?

Top Ten Excuses for Why I Can't Go on a Mission Trip

"I'm Not Talented Enough"

It can be very easy to be envious of someone else's gifts, talents, and abilities. There are so many talented people out there, and when we get stuck in the mind-set of comparing ourselves to others – it drags us down even further. Below is a typical conversation I have on a fairly regular basis...

> **Student**: I'm not sure I should go into ministry.
>
> **Me**: Why not?
>
> **Student**: Because I'm not like so-and-so (their idealized "perfect minister" role model, or another ministry student who they are comparing themselves to).
>
> **Me**: Good! I don't need another one of those... I already *have* one! I need you to be who God's dreamed you to be!

God has equipped you with the perfect gifts to accomplish the things He's called you to do! As Ephesians 2:10 reminds us, He has already prepared "good works" for us to do. So, we can be confident that we have just the right amount of talent to do them!

"I Don't Know What to Say"

Few things are worse than awkward silence. The fear of not knowing what to say can be a crippling one. I've heard that public speaking is one of the top fears of Americans. The good news for followers of Jesus is that He gives us all the words we need (Matthew 10:19-20). I can't tell you how many times I've been talking with a non-Christian and felt like I didn't know what to say, and yet somehow the words just came. God provides.

Moses had this fear. And God certainly provided for him! But notice that before Moses got more comfortable with speaking, God told him to have his brother Aaron speak for him (Exodus 4:14-15). If you're uncomfortable speaking or feel you don't know what to say, I would bet that God has put an "Aaron" in your life to help you.

I also wonder if we put a little too much emphasis on speaking. Sometimes the best thing to say is… nothing. Sometimes the best thing to do is just listen. Many attribute this piece of wisdom to St. Francis of Assisi: "Preach the Gospel at all times, and if necessary, use words." No words required. All of us can do that!

"I'm Too Busy"

Isn't it funny how sometimes time goes so slowly and other times it goes so quickly? There isn't anything we can do to stop time, and none of us knows how much time we have left here on earth. Even with all of our technology and time-saving gadgets, we seem to have less available time in our lives than ever before. We can barely fit in time for our family and friends – so how are we supposed to take a week or two off work for a mission trip? Our lives and our calendars are packed full!

King Solomon talks quite a bit about time in Ecclesiastes. Chapter 3 is arguably the most famous section of the book, where we are reminded that there is a time for everything, and he provides the familiar list. But later in Ecclesiastes he continues the discussion on time. For example, in Ecclesiastes 8:5 he writes: **"the wise heart will know the proper time and procedure."** There will always be time for the things we prioritize and value.

Maybe there could be a way to "double dip" with your mission trip. If you've been meaning to spend more quality time with your spouse, children, or parents, taking a mission trip together would be a powerful, life-changing family getaway! Students may find that they can use their mission trip experience for school reports or other assignments. Look for creative ways to tie a missional adventure into some of your other life goals and priorities, and you will find it is much easier to schedule it in!

So if you value missions – if you believe that God's love is truly for the whole world, and that He can use you in powerful ways to communicate that love – then you will find the time. Your time is the most valuable thing you have, and to give it away to others is a beautiful gift!

Personal Mission Perspective

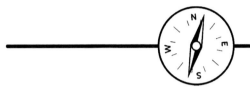

A Change In Perspective
by Emily Eltiste

As a kid, I really was not exposed to a whole lot of hardships. I lived in Orange County, California, went to a private school, and had a roof over my head and food for every meal. I am blessed to be able to say that I never had to experience what it is like to go without. When I got to high school, I was heavily involved in our church youth group, and was given the opportunity to go on several mission trips. Let me tell you – there is nothing like a mission trip to pop an Orange County kid's bubble. I am so grateful for the time I spent in New Zealand, Alaska, and on the Apache Indian Reservation in Arizona. I was able to see the world beyond my narrow scope, and gain a whole new appreciation for the hurts and struggles of people all over the world. It also made me appreciate so much more the blessings I had back at home.

When I think back on those trips, so many memories come flooding back – but Apache stories seem to stand out the most. As I'm sure you can gather from the other stories in this book, Apache is a place that is very near and dear to the hearts of those who have spent time there. When you go on a trip to Apache, you never know what might happen, but you *do* know that God is going to work in mighty ways. The

Apache people know pain and suffering like no other group
of people I have worked with. They deal with poverty,
alcoholism, and death on a daily basis. Yet, when you sit in
one of their worship services, you see them praising God with
more enthusiasm and gusto than in any church I had ever
been to. It was a huge wake-up call for me, on my first trip to
Apache, to witness just how little these families have. I
remember going over to one family's home where our team
was going to do an "extreme makeover" on the house. We
painted the outside, re-did their roof, and did some repair
work inside. I remember walking into the house and feeling
so guilty that their entire house was not much bigger than my
bedroom back at home. Another eye-opener was how many
kids were left alone during the day. I have always loved being
around kids and working with them, so to see so many left
without supervision or proper care broke my heart. One of my
favorite parts of the trip was when we were able to play with
the kids or just bring them some new toys. I think Apache has
become such a special place to many of us because we can
see God working there in so many different ways. We can
only do so much to serve them in the weeks that we spend
there, but we know He will continue to care for them more
than we ever could. There's a lot of need, but God is using
people like Pastor Reno (their local pastor) and other mission
teams to bring some hope and assurance to the Apache
people.

As I mentioned previously, I had the opportunity to go on a
mission trip to New Zealand as well. This trip was much
different than Apache, but still gave me some new
perspectives on life beyond Southern California. The people
of St. Luke's Lutheran Church in Palmerston North, New
Zealand were not all that different than the people in my
home congregation of St. Paul's Lutheran Church in Orange,
California. St. Luke's had Sunday School classes and a youth

group and worship services just like back home. We spent our time there leading VBS activities and helping with worship services. We built relationships and served the best we could as a group of teenagers. The perspective I gained on this trip wasn't due to physical and social hardships like in Apache, but instead it was that we were able to see that there were Christian teens, just like us, all over the world. I don't think I fully grasped how important our time in New Zealand was until about a year later when St. Luke's pastor, Pastor Greg, came to visit our church in California and shared his thoughts on our time spent with his congregation. Among other things, he told us that our time in New Zealand had inspired their youth group to go out and do mission work. It was incredibly powerful for us to hear that the time we spent leading games, singing songs, cooking meals, and building relationships had inspired others to go out and do the same.

After high school, I went on to study Christian Education at Concordia University in Irvine, CA. I am now serving as the Director of Christian Education at a church in Northern California. I can honestly say that I don't think I would be where I am today if it weren't for the experiences I had in the mission field. I learned how to serve others and serve God by stepping outside of my comfort zone. I cannot wait to take the youth I work with on a mission trip, so that they can also experience this change of perspective for themselves.

· · · · ·

Emily Eltiste currently serves as the Director of Christian Education at Bethany Lutheran Church in Vacaville, CA. She considers herself fortunate to have spent her high school years being mentored by Jake Youmans. She lovingly "blames" him for getting her into the wonderful world of church work!

Personal Mission Perspective

All She Had
by Lydia Humphries

But a poor widow came and put in two very small copper coins, worth only a few cents. Calling his disciples to him, Jesus said, "Truly I tell you, this poor widow has put more into the treasury than all the others. They all gave out of their wealth; but she, out of her poverty, put in everything – all she had to live on." (Mark 12:42-44)

For over eight months now, I have been blessed to live and work in missions on the White Mountain Apache Indian Reservation in northeastern Arizona. This place has been transformational in the lives of many – not only those who were served by the mission teams, but also those who were serving.

On the few mission trips I had attended to the Rez beforehand, I had seen transformation happen in the hearts of our team when we realized we were receiving far more than we could ever give. That moment of realization hits us when people who live in poverty bring us gifts of all sorts, typically in the form of food. They are giving out of the little that they have. Having experienced that moment before, and seeing others experience it, I had not expected to be shocked and touched if something similar happened.

Some of my greatest relationships have been with older ladies who are rarely reached by most people. They stick to themselves. This generation has been my favorite to grow, laugh, eat, cook, and sew with. I've realized how much these ladies love me because every time I go out of town, they fervently ask when I'll return! I have to assure them that I would not leave without letting them know.

One evening, before I left for Christmas break, I was making the rounds and saying my "see ya later's" when one little lady, about 85 years old, blind in one eye, and with the most cheerful and touching smile, slipped something in my hand. In the hug, she whispered, "This is for gas. Please use it." Of course, I protested. Money? I have some money! And beyond that, I'm supposed to give things to *you*! It was toward the end of the month, and I was fairly certain this woman was on Social Security, which is deposited on the first or after. This meant that most of her income was likely gone. I was weighed with guilt – surely I could not take this woman's money – yet surely I could not shame her by forcing her to take it back. As I struggled with this internally for what felt like hours (though it was truly minutes) she took my hand again and closed my fingers around the bill. Her actions led me to be so unsure' of what I would find when I opened my fist in my car.

When I finally unclenched my hand and looked at the bill, I saw ten dollars. Ten dollars at the end of the month, from a woman who is elderly and poor. Those ten dollars meant so much to me, and were so much more meaningful than any monetary gift I've ever been given. It took me a moment to collect myself, and I was later reminded of Jesus' words in

Mark 12:44 – **"They all gave out of their wealth; but she, out of her poverty, put in everything – all she had to live on."** Sometimes, when we come to give out of our abundance, that's when we see that we are constantly being served.

. . . . .

Lydia Humphries is from Spring, Texas and went to school at Concordia University Texas. Formerly, she thought God was leading her to be involved in missions in India, and now jests that the lines were crossed and she missed a few letters because she now works as a missionary intern on the White Mountain Apache INDIAN reservation! She is enjoying her time, and cannot wait to see what else God has in store!

Ends of the Earth

Introduction to Ends of the Earth

This one is the most self-explanatory. Literally and metaphorically, Ends of the Earth is, well, the ends of the earth... It is every corner of the earth. It is every tongue and every tribe on the planet. Throughout the Scriptures, we see that God's love is for the whole world.

This one might require you to travel – plane, train, or automobile – your choice. And this one is definitely going to require you to meet people not just different from you – but *very* different from you: different languages, different cultures, different in nearly every way. But even though things will be different, you will also get to explore some of the things that are similar among the people of the world. You will learn the power of a smile and nonverbal communication – even wacky hand-motion-sign-language-communication. You will learn that family is a universal value, and can also cause the greatest pain in one's life. You will learn that just because there is a lack of financial resources does not mean there is a lack of joy. You will learn that love really is a universal language.

And just in case you get car/train/plane-induced motion sickness – I have good news for you too. God is bringing the world to you! In the larger cities in the U.S.: Los Angeles, Houston, New York, Chicago, etc., there are hundreds of different languages spoken. Even the smaller, more rural towns in North America are becoming more culturally diverse. Because of the unchurched population here in the U.S., we're the third largest mission field in the world behind China and India! In fact, I have met people from countries as far away as Korea who are coming *here* to serve as missionaries… in North America!

The Ends of the Earth could be at the end of your street! Let's explore what it means to be a witness to the Ends of the Earth.

Music

I come from a fairly long line of musicians. My mother is a choir director and church organist. My brother is a composer. My grandfather was a master accordion player... and no – that's not a joke! And while I am certainly not a talented musician myself, I appreciate music and how it's made. Music is one of those things that unites a culture and can bridge gaps between different cultures. I've been told that every culture on the planet has some kind of musical expression. While one can easily appreciate the beauty of some music, other forms seem to be more of an acquired taste. But one thing is certain of all music – someone thinks it's beautiful or they wouldn't have created it. Music tells our stories. Music moves us emotionally and causes us to think and reflect. It touches our hearts deeply, in ways that nothing else can.

As Martin Luther said, "next to the Word of God, music deserves the highest praise. ... After all, the gift of language combined with the gift of song was only given to man to let him know that he should praise God with both word and music, namely, by proclaiming [the Word of God] through music."[6] God's love and grace can be communicated beautifully through music. Think about the diversity of worship music in our North American culture. We have songs based on the Torah which is about 3,500 years old. We have songs based on the Psalms which range from about 3,500 to

about 2,500 years old. We have songs based on the Gospels
and Epistles which are about 2,000 years old. And somehow
we continue to have gifted musicians who take those ancient
words and make them feel fresh! Music is timely and
timeless.

On a trip to Hong Kong, I was fortunate to work with some of
their government subsidized schools. The public schools in
Hong Kong are run by various organizations, and the
Lutheran Church-Hong Kong Synod actually runs several
government-funded schools! They get to teach about Jesus in
their curriculum – and the government pays for it! It's a
fascinating model.

During this time, I saw missionaries share Jesus in bold and
practical ways through teaching English and building cross-
cultural relationships. As I visited the different departments
of the school, I was fascinated by the music room. It was
filled with beautiful, traditional Chinese instruments, many of
which I had never seen before. The students were so excited
to show me each of the instruments and how it worked, and
they even let me try to play some of them! I don't remember
what all of the instruments were called, but there were several
stringed instruments, including one with only one string! It is
played with a bow similar to a violin but is held like a stand-
up bass, even though it's smaller than a guitar... I found it
impossible to produce pleasant sounds with it, but the
students at the school seemed to have no problem whatso-
ever!

Being a lover of music, I was delighted when they gave me
an impromptu concert. The students smiled proudly as they
got a chance to show off their musical skills. And they did an
absolutely beautiful job! I thanked the students for playing for
me and then asked the music teacher if they ever played in

church. "Oh no!" she said. "These instruments are for Chinese music, not Christian music!"

Perhaps something got lost in translation, as tends to happen with their pretty good English and my horrible Chinese. But I think there is something bigger at play here. I really believe that someone, somewhere down the line told them that "this" is Chinese and "that" is Christian, and that there is no blending of the two cultures. The music teacher seemed to have clean and clear compartments for what is Chinese and what is Christian. Someone probably told them that an organ is the only acceptable instrument with which to play Christian music. (In fact, the organ was the only instrument that was used on the few Sundays I visited their church.) The message was that Chinese instruments do not belong in church.

This breaks my heart! God loves culture! Otherwise, why would He have created so many diverse cultures? Look at the world – God loves variety! Listen to St. Paul in Philippians 2:9-11 –

> **Therefore God exalted him (Jesus) to the highest place and gave him the name that is above every name, that at the name of Jesus every knee should bow, in heaven and on earth and under the earth, and every tongue acknowledge that Jesus Christ is Lord, to the glory of God the Father.**

The word "tongue" means so much more than the piece of fleshy muscle that resides in your mouth. It's about language. It's about culture. It's about all the unique ethnic groups around the globe. God wants all people in the world to confess Jesus as Lord and Savior, and He rejoices when they do so within the context of their own beautiful and unique culture.

What if a church in Hong Kong actually used Chinese instruments to play Christian songs? What do you think people would say? I think it would reach out to people who would never otherwise step into an organ-playing church. Maybe it would help connect them with the Gospel in their own "tongue." As we look at what it means to be missional, let's strive to communicate the Gospel message through the various "instruments" found in each group's own unique culture. By taking time to explore their culture first, we can then show them how Jesus connects!

I had another interesting but quite different experience involving music on our very first trip to Apache. As we toured the church sanctuary, we noticed a rather large electric organ proudly displayed in the front corner of the worship center. I found this to be very curious as music, rhythm, and dance are such prominent parts of their culture. Would they celebrate with their cultural instruments and then worship in church with a European-looking organ? After experiencing two worship gatherings, it became clear that the organ was not a standard part of their worship expression. They used guitars, and most significantly lots of drums and rhythm instruments. I was intrigued that nearly half of the congregation brought their own tambourine to worship! They sang songs I had heard before, although not done in the same way. They focused more on rhythm than melody, which is very fitting to their culture.

After several years, I asked Pastor Reno about the organ and if they ever used it. "No," he said. "We've never used it. But someone off the Rez thought that in order to be a church, we should have an organ. So they brought us one and it sits over there." Praise God that the Apache people realize that their own culture, instruments, and music can serve in worship to Jesus!

Think about your own culture and how it can uniquely impact worship. Do you even know what your culture is? Asking someone about their culture is like asking a fish about water... The response is: "What's water?" It can be challenging to see our own culture because it's all we know. It surrounds us, and until we step out of it we may not fully realize what it is. God's story of redemption and grace translates into any culture. We just need to look for the connecting points, and perhaps music is a great place to start.

Questions for Reflection and Discussion

1. What does music mean to you? How have you seen music used powerfully in ministry?

2. What is your culture? How do you know it's your culture?

3. How can you use music as a way to connect other cultures to Jesus?

"I Hate God"

Whenever I teach, preach, speak, serve as master of ceremonies, or generally work a crowd, I love audience participation and interaction. The more the better! I love questions. I love comments. I even love tangents, as they can lead to powerful teachable moments – for the students *and* for me! We all learn more when we become actively involved.

But in all my years of teaching, the most memorable comment from the crowd came from a five-year-old girl in Palmerston North, New Zealand. Our mission group was doing a Bible School lesson during a VBS-type event during their winter break… in July! (Winter in July was a new experience for us!) There were about 25 kids gathered for the lesson that day, ranging from ages four to ten. The kids were all very excited to have some crazy Americans with their crazy accents visiting their church! Everyone seemed happy to be there, and our VBS was off to a very positive start.

At one point during the Bible lesson, a little girl raised her hand. We called on her, and she said: "I hate God." I glanced around the room, and all of my youth had their mouths wide open, staring at her in disbelief. For a moment, everyone was silent. You could have heard a pin drop. Then all of their eyes turned to me, asking by non-verbal communication: *What do we do now?!*

Looking back on this moment, perhaps the most stunning part was that she actually raised her hand just to tell us this! It seems like a rather polite way to make a rude comment. But before I could even think of what to say, Corey – a six foot six, smiling, floppy-haired, lanky high school senior – walked over to her and picked her up. Without saying a word, he put her on his lap. We then continued on with the lesson, right where we had left off. A smile started to form on the girl's face.

For the next few days, Corey and this little girl, Amy, were inseparable. She was constantly riding on his shoulders with hands in the air, obviously never having felt that big and important before! Little Amy was actually able to get the basketball into the hoop from that height! Corey was the drummer in our praise band and, sure enough, he drummed with Amy sitting on his shoulders – which was rather impressive to watch.

Amy was a kid from the community, not from the church. But the church members knew who she was, as her mom took full advantage of many of the church's programs, mostly for the free babysitting. All of the people who knew Amy, including her mother, said they could not believe how well-behaved she was with us and how much joy it brought her spending time with Corey. Corey didn't judge her. Corey made her feel special. With him, she left loved. She never said it, but she didn't have to. It was written all over her face!

One of our traditions on mission trips is to give each member of the team a Bible that they are to give away to someone who impacted them during the trip. Ideally, the Bible would go to someone who didn't have one. But that is merely a suggestion, not a requirement. It's more about relationships and showing value to people who impact you. On the final day of our trip, Corey gave his Bible to Amy. She just started weeping. Corey had not experienced this before, so he asked her what was wrong. She wiped the tears away and through them said, "No one's ever given me a Bible before!"

I thanked Corey for befriending Amy, and asked him what inspired him to go over to her after her "I hate God" comment. I was very curious about his thought process. What he had done with Amy looked almost instinctive. And the timing could not have been better for those instincts to kick in! His response to my question? "I don't know." How reassuring and humbling it is that God can use us, even when we don't know *why* we do what we do!

It's a *Beauty and the Beast* kind of story. It's a story of the goofy high school kid and the "unlovable" little girl from opposite ends of the world coming together in the name of Jesus. Since that trip, they haven't seen each other again – and most likely never will – but I know the encounter lingers in them both. And the image of unconditional love, of a little girl who hates God on the shoulders of a teenager who loves God with all his heart, is one that will stick in my mind forever.

· · · · ·

In the Gospel of John, the author refers to himself as **"the disciple whom Jesus loved"** (John 21:20-24). And while this may sound cocky, it was also the truth. John and Jesus had a special relationship. Most scholars think that John was the youngest of the disciples, part of the "inner circle" of Peter, James, and himself. In his letters, 1 John, 2 John, and 3 John, he expands on this theme of love. He says in 1 John 4:7 – **"let us love one another."** Why should we love others? Let's face it – some people seem downright unlovable. Some people push our buttons and antagonize us. Some people are really, really hard to love! John's statement sounds like one of those ideals that just isn't very practical in real life. But John answers the *Why?* question right away. In verse 19 he says: **"We love because he first loved us."** It's not about whether or not someone is kind, or cooperative, or enjoyable to be around. It's all about Jesus' love. *His* love is the only reason that we can love anyone!

John then gets even bolder, and in verse 21 says: **"Anyone who loves God must also love their brother and sister."** Jesus' love is the inspiration, and empowers us to love others. Note that loving others isn't really a choice for us. John says it's a "must," if we love God. Maybe Corey's answer of "I don't know" is the right answer after all. He loved Amy because Jesus first loved him – and that's all he really needed to know. As St. John says in 1 John 4:12 – **"if we love one another, God lives in us and his love is made complete in us."** The completeness of His love comes when we let His love for us overflow onto those around us! The indwelling of God cannot stay in us. It must move through us to touch other people's lives as well.

Perhaps the reason the world so often says "I hate God" is that they have never experienced Jesus' love through others. Maybe they have heard about it, but they haven't experienced it in a nonjudgmental way that makes them *feel* loved. Often love is best expressed through our actions, and not merely through our words. Or perhaps we have tried to love the world in a way they cannot connect with. Amy had heard many Bible lessons and stories, but it didn't become real to her until Corey picked her up and put her on his shoulders. In order to live life as a mission trip, we must find ways to connect with people – to love them in a way they will respond to.

Dr. Gary Chapman wrote a book called *The Five Love Languages*. In it, he suggests that all human beings essentially give and receive love in five different ways: physical touch, quality time, gifts, acts of service, and words of affirmation. If we really want to show our love for someone, Dr. Chapman explains, the key is to love that individual in the way that he or she prefers to receive love – not in the way that we may prefer to *give* love. For example, my wife's love language is words of affirmation, but for the first few years of marriage I would show her love through gifts. Her lack of appreciation for these gifts drove us both crazy. It turned out that gifts are actually her least preferred "love language." But once I figured out the best way to share my gestures of love with her, everything changed for the better!

What I find fascinating about these five "love languages" is that God has shown His love to us through all these different ways! If your love language is physical touch, God provides the Sacraments of Baptism and Holy Communion where we can actually feel His love and taste His forgiveness in a tangible way. For those who feel most loved through quality time, Matthew's Gospel ends with that promise: **"And surely I am with you always, to the very end of the age."** (Matthew 28:20) Do you prefer gifts as a demonstration of love? Grace is the very best gift of all! Or as James sums it up in James 1:17, **"Every good and perfect gift is from above, coming down from the Father of the heavenly lights, who does not change like shifting shadows."** For those who rather receive love through acts of service, there is nothing greater than the sacrifice that Jesus made on the cross for each one of us. And if someone is looking for words of affirmation, the Bible is a pretty good place to find God's incredible and boundless love spoken tenderly and encouragingly to us!

When we love someone in the way they prefer to be loved, the barriers that stand between us will come down. But finding out how someone wants to be loved takes time and effort. It means putting aside our own preconceptions, ideas, and preferences, and fully tuning into the needs of the other person. But as we strive to live a missional life, it is worth the effort to discover the best ways to connect to another person's heart. As we do, God will show us opportunities to reach out to them with His love!

Questions for Reflection and Discussion

1. What is your first reaction when you meet someone who hates God? Do you scorn them? Avoid them? Or embrace them? Why?

2. How can you befriend and show love to someone who may hate God?

3. Which love language do you prefer to receive? Which one(s) do you seem to demonstrate most naturally toward others?

Thai Bible

On a trip to Thailand that I took with my wife Christy a number of years ago, one of the highlights for us was a worship service at an international church. The people were from all over the world. The pastor was Canadian, the worship leader was Australian, and we met parishioners from India, Pakistan, China, Thailand, and even another person from the U.S.! We had never experienced anything quite like this before – or since! It truly felt like the Great Commission being lived out, with people from around the world coming together to praise and glory the one true God! It will always be one of the worship highlights of my life!

This fellow American happened to be sitting in front of us, and when he recognized that we were visitors he offered us a precious gift. He gave us a Bible that is both in Thai and English. He explained that whenever he meets another American, he always gives them this particular type of Bible as a souvenir of their time in Thailand. I love this Bible! This has inspired me on all of my subsequent international travels to try to get a Bible that is in the native language. So far, I have collected Bibles in Mandarin Chinese, German, Hawaiian (and Hawaiian Pidgin!), Spanish, and Apache.

The man who gave us the Thai Bible also included his business card and encouraged us to keep in touch with him. I regretfully admit that I failed do so. But one day, about eight years after that trip to Thailand, something happened that reconnected us. Kathy Borg, the secretary at the church I served in Southern California, told me of a new friend of hers who was from Thailand and had recently moved to the United States. Kathy had been developing a relationship with the owner of a new Thai restaurant and in their conversations the owner expressed an openness to Christianity – but she could not find a Bible in Thai. So, Kathy asked if I had any idea where to find one.

Wow! Did I know where to find one? I happened to have one on the shelf in my office! So of course I gave it to her, she gave it to her friend, and her friend became a follower of Jesus. What a blessing – but certainly not a coincidence – that I happened to have a Thai Bible lying around!

Well, I immediately e-mailed my old friend in Thailand to tell him the story of his gift Bible, and he was so excited. He expressed how God knew he needed to hear something like this that day, as he was rather down in his faith and needed the boost that such an affirming story like this provides. It was obvious God was at work in so many different ways, all centered around the gift of God's Word.

One of my favorite and one of the most practical websites is www.biblegateway.com. There are so many different English translations of the Bible, and this website has over a hundred versions just in English! Here you can also find the Bible available in over fifty languages, from Amharic (I'm not even sure where in the world they speak that language!) to Vietnamese. This website also has audio Bibles that you can download or live stream for free.

We live in an incredible time where the Bible is accessible to almost everyone! My sister is hearing impaired, so I have always been fascinated by churches that offer a "signing ministry" to meet the needs of the deaf. My aunt and uncle spent years volunteering with a Braille ministry that enables the visually impaired to read the Word of God. There are Bible apps available for your smartphone that can be downloaded faster than you can say "John 3:16!" As I remind my students, a book is a form of technology. Who knows all the amazing and innovative ways through which we will be able to access God's Word in the future!

Here in our country, an English Bible is so easy to find – there is even a free copy in just about every hotel room in the country! Because they are so easily accessible for us, we tend to take them for granted. Believe it or not, there are still thousands of languages that do not have a Biblical translation yet. And there are still many places in the world where owning a Bible can get you thrown in jail or even killed. How blessed we are to have such access to God's Word!

· · · · ·

The Bible is the Word of God. All Christians know the power of the Word of God is life-changing – it's a double-edged sword according to Scripture (cf. Hebrews 4:12). But what if we can't understand what we are reading? In Acts 8:29-31, we have an excerpt from the account of Philip and an Ethiopian who is searching for answers from God's Word:

> **The Spirit told Philip, "Go to that chariot and stay near it."**
>
> **Then Philip ran up to the chariot and heard the man reading Isaiah the prophet. "Do you understand what you are reading?" Philip asked.**

"How can I," he said, "unless someone explains it to me?" So he invited Philip to come up and sit with him.

We need to hear God's Word in our own language – both literally and figuratively – or we will struggle unnecessarily to understand it. When being missional, how can you speak the Word of God in the language of those you are serving? Literally, you can give them the Word of God – a tangible Bible in their native language – from a Christian organization such as Multi-Language Media, Inc. (www.multilanguage. com). And figuratively, you can take it a step further by explaining God's Word to them in such a way that they take the message to heart. Maybe God will use you as He used Philip – to connect Scripture to someone's life, right where they happen to be!

I always keep a Bible in my car. You never know when there will be a Bible emergency! And over the years, those Bibles have come in very handy, as I have given many of them away when I have had the privilege of meeting and connecting with different people. As American Express® used to say: "Don't leave home without it!" What if we had the same attitude about the Word of God? The Bible – don't be anywhere without it!

Questions for Reflection and Discussion

1. Have you experienced worship in a different language? If so, what was it like? If not, where could you go to experience this in your community?

2. What does your copy of the Bible mean to you?

3. What different forms of the Bible do you use regularly? (Examples: hardcover book, online Bible, Bible app on an iPad, etc.) When do you primarily use each one?

4. Have you ever given away a Bible? If not, can you think of someone you could give one to?

A Little Bit Bolder

Of all the mission trips I have participated in, I would have to say that the most personally impactful one was the opportunity to work with the persecuted underground church in North Africa. Now, before I begin this story, I should explain that I need to be intentionally vague about the people I worked with and the places we visited. Missionaries have been deported or even killed due to well-meaning church groups mentioning specifics about their locations and identities. For these missionaries, this is truly a life or death situation. While they are not afraid of death, they feel called to be wary so they can continue ministering to the people in spite of the dangerous risks involved.

On our last day in a North African country, our team was doing some prayer-walking around the city and then out to a pier that overlooked the beautiful area. I'm not sure if you've ever prayer-walked before – many people haven't – but it is very simple. We walk and we pray. We pray for who and what we see as we walk along. It's simple but also very profound and impacting. God reveals things about His plan constantly as you walk and pray. It's inspired by one of the shortest verses in the Bible – **"pray continually"** (1 Thessalonians 5:17). One of the local missionaries and I were praying, talking, and sharing our stories as we walked along.

He was 26 at the time and I was a few years older. He grew up a Muslim in Egypt. While it was not illegal to be a Christian in Egypt (about 10% of the population is Coptic – and you can tell who they are by the mandatory cross tattoo on their right wrist), it was very illegal to *convert* to Christianity from Islam. He had grown up as a devout Muslim, but loved to ask questions. In his teenage years, he encountered a Christian missionary who showed him the *real* Jesus – not the Isa that he had heard was just a prophet – but Jesus, the Son of God and the true Savior of the World.

He was 16 when he became a fully devoted follower of Jesus. At first, he did not tell his parents out of fear of what they would do. But eventually he felt compelled to tell them the changes he had experienced, and he invited them to follow Jesus too. When they heard this, they were furious. They kicked him out of the house and out of the family. They basically had a funeral for him and considered him "dead," even though he was now alive like never before! Fearing for his life, he fled the country and ended up in the country that we were now visiting. He initially found work as a tour guide, and eventually got involved in the underground church and now serves as a missionary. He has not had any contact with his family for years. He truly had to sacrifice them for the sake of the Gospel.

I really only had one question for him – even though I asked many more. (I do love asking questions!) I feel as though in America, it is so easy for us to take our freedom of religion for granted. We lose sight of the fact that persecution is still very real for so many of our fellow believers around the world. And so I asked him, "Are you ever afraid for your life?" This was the first time I ever encountered someone who truly had a reason to be, because of their faith.

He paused for a second or two before responding, and then answered very quietly, "Yes, daily." He then went on to tell me stories of brothers and sisters in the faith who sacrificed their lives for the work of sharing the Gospel. (In fact, two weeks after our team was safely back home, we got a correspondence that some friends of his in Iran, a husband and wife missionary team, had disappeared – never to be heard from again.) He told me story after story of lives that had been lost for the sake of the Gospel. His eyes filled with tears as he remembered his friends and celebrated that they are now home with Jesus for all eternity. I think it was therapeutic for him to tell these stories. It was certainly powerful for us to hear them.

But then he shared something that has changed my prayer life forever. As he was discussing the reality that "they" could come in at any moment and drag him away, he talked about how he moves forward despite such knowledge in the back of his mind. He said, "Every morning for the ten years I've been a Christian, my first prayer in the morning is, 'Lord, make me a little bit bolder.' And every day He does."

A little bit bolder. What would happen in your life if that was your daily morning prayer? The temptations and challenges that you face at school or work – *Lord, make me a little bit bolder.* The coworker who doesn't know Jesus – *Lord, make me a little bit bolder.* Parenting in truth and love – *Lord, make me a little bit bolder.* How bold could Jesus make you? As Jesus said, **"Ask and it will be given to you"** (Matthew 7:7). God is faithful, and He will strengthen you just as you ask Him. But if you were to pray for boldness, do you really know what you would be praying for?

· · · · ·

Joshua had one of the most difficult jobs in all of Scripture. He had to follow in Moses' footsteps! Moses – who parted the Red Sea (Exodus 14:15-22). Moses – who struck a rock in the desert and water came out (Exodus 17:1-6). Moses – who boldly took down Pharaoh (Exodus 12:29-33 and 14:23-31), the most powerful person in history to that point, and who many people considered a diety! Joshua had to pick up the reins after an incredible leader. Talk about a hard act to follow! I love the contrast between Moses parting the Red Sea and Joshua crossing the Jordon (Joshua 3). Moses seemed so bold and confident, stretching out his hand over the sea, and the sea parted (Exodus 14:21). But for Joshua, it's a different story. The people have to start walking in the water, and *then* the river parts (Joshua 3:15-16). They get wet, and then they get dry land. What would Moses think about that?! I like to think this is essentially God's way of telling Joshua that he's the leader now... but he's not going to be Moses!

In Joshua chapter 1, God informs Joshua that Moses is dead and that he himself is the new leader. In so doing, God tells Joshua: **"Be strong and courageous. Do not be afraid; do not be discouraged, for the LORD your God will be with you wherever you go."** (verse 9) The encouragement to be strong and courageous is a recurring theme at the end of Deuteronomy and in Joshua. Moses tells it to Joshua (Deuteronomy 31:7), God tells it to Joshua (Deuteronomy 31:23 and Joshua 1:6-9), and then Joshua tells it to the people (Joshua 10:25). In other words, God tells Joshua to be a little bit bolder every day. And Joshua was! After 40 years of wandering, the people finally obtained the Promised Land.

At the end of Joshua's life – after a lifetime of asking God to make him bolder, and striving to be strong and courageous –

the Israelites are at a crossroads. Joshua's last speech to them is recorded in Joshua chapter 24. In verses 14-15, he says:

> **Now fear the LORD and serve him with all faithfulness. Throw away the gods your ancestors worshiped beyond the Euphrates River and in Egypt, and serve the LORD. But if serving the LORD seems undesirable to you, then choose for yourselves this day whom you will serve, whether the gods your ancestors served beyond the Euphrates, or the gods of the Amorites, in whose land you are living. But as for me and my household, we will serve the LORD.**

This is Joshua's final act of boldness. He has passed his faith onto his children and grandchildren. He has fought the good fight and finished the race (cf. 2 Timothy 4:7). His life has been one of service and boldness.

The people grab hold of that boldness! What is their response? They proclaim in Joshua 24:24: **"We will serve the LORD our God and obey him."** Boldness is contagious and inspiring. When you ask for personal boldness, you are not just blessing yourself but everyone you come in contact with. Boldness from Jesus causes you to be more of a servant.

As you contemplate boldness, think about it in three areas: thoughts, words, and deeds. It all starts with our thoughts. Think bold thoughts! Dream bold dreams. A funny thing happens when we think boldly – the thoughts don't stay in our head! To think bold thoughts, start by heeding the call of Hebrews 3:1 – **"fix your thoughts on Jesus."**

Then consider boldness when it comes to our words. We should be bold in Jesus' love and grace in how we speak.

This requires us to choose our words carefully – to think before we speak and always to speak the truth in love (cf. Ephesians 4:15). And sometimes we can be bold in what we *don't* say – in biting our tongue. As St. James puts it: **"Those who consider themselves religious and yet do not keep a tight rein on their tongues deceive themselves, and their religion is worthless."** (James 1:26)

Then consider boldness in terms of deeds. Your actions should be bold. Doing bold things means doing the selfless thing. It means doing the difficult thing. Again, the boldness comes both in what we do (**"For we are God's handiwork, created in Christ Jesus to do good works"** – Ephesians 2:10) and in what we *don't* do (**"turn to them the other cheek"** – Matthew 5:39).

If this sounds a bit intimidating, remember – think baby steps. What I love about this prayer is that we're asking God to make us "a little bit bolder," a little more every single day, as we trust and follow Him. Praying for boldness is one of the keys to living life as a mission trip. We cannot truly live a missional life without boldness in our hearts and courage in our words. *Lord, make me a little bit bolder!*

Questions for Reflection and Discussion

1. Do you know anyone who has suffered persecution for their faith? Have you ever experienced persecution even on a much smaller scale (such as bullying, shunning, verbal insults, or inequitable treatment)?

2. What do you think would happen if you prayed, "Lord, make me a little bit bolder?"

3. How can you become bolder in your thoughts? In your words? In your deeds?

4. Is it possible to be too bold? Why or why not?

Top Ten Excuses for Why I Can't Go on a Mission Trip

"I Don't Feel Called to Go"

Some people in ministry want to undervalue the role of "feelings" in our relationship with Jesus. But my response is, "Then why did God give them to us?" We certainly need to guard our feelings the same way we need to guard our mind. But feelings are valid.

A call from God is a very serious thing. When people say "God told me" to do something, I believe them, as long as it's not against Scripture. I'm a little more hesitant to believe them when they say God told them that *I* (me, Jacob Youmans) should do something; but that's a different story!

St. Paul – who knows a thing or two about being called by God – makes it clear in Ephesians 4:1-7 that all followers of Jesus are called to faith and **"to live a life worthy of the calling you have received"** (verse 1). But the question remains – what if you don't *feel* called to go on that mission trip? First and foremost, pray about it! Seek the counsel of wise people. I also believe it's important to err on the side of being **"fools for Christ"** (1 Corinthians 4:10). Meaning, even if you don't have "that feeling" you would expect, or it seems illogical, and yet it's a selfless act that benefits others – then give it a shot! My advice to students wrestling with two choices is – pick the most selfless thing! That's usually what God's called us to!

"I'm Afraid"

There are so many things you could be afraid of on a mission trip. Travel itself can be very dangerous. Cars, planes, and trains can crash. People can get killed even while walking! There is no completely safe way to travel. Different places have different diseases. I don't think I've been on even one international trip where someone's stomach didn't get upset. People speaking a foreign language could be making fun of you, right in front of your face, and you wouldn't even know it!

I'm guessing that there are many things you now enjoy and are passionate about that at one time scared you. But once you overcame that fear, you were free to truly enjoy the beauty and wonder of that activity. Fear can be conquered – it's not the end. The first thing the risen Jesus said is: **"Greetings … Do not be afraid."** (Matthew 28:9-10) That's how He calls us to live – without fear! While there is a fine line between careful and careless, the call is to *fear not*. If your fear is stifling you or interfering with your ministry opportunities, talk to people who have done what you are afraid to do. If you are nervous about the unknown – try it once and see how it goes. But as people of God, we cannot allow fear to win!

"People Need Jesus Here; I Don't Need to Go Anywhere"

I've heard this excuse thousands of times, and on the surface it's difficult to argue with this logic. It's so important that we reach out to people here. Our neighbors, family, friends, etc. – they all need to know about the life-changing good news of Jesus!

But the problem comes in the narrow mind-set. While, yes, people here need Jesus, we cannot forget about the people here, there, and everywhere. The calling to follow Jesus is so much bigger than just my little world – because God loves the whole world! When we don't go, and instead just focus on whatever is right in front of us, it can stunt our growth. When we don't go, we can forget just how big God is, because it's a big world... and God's even bigger! Traveling out of our immediate area (and out of our comfort zone) opens up our minds to see just how big the task at hand really is.

In Mark chapter 1, we see Jesus starting His ministry. He began healing many people and preaching the good news. People were amazed and drawn to Him. In fact, the Scriptures say the whole town gathered at the door of the home where He was staying. Mark then tells us,

> **Very early in the morning, while it was still dark, Jesus got up, left the house and went off to a**

solitary place, where he prayed. Simon and his companions went to look for him, and when they found him, they exclaimed: "Everyone is looking for you!" Jesus replied, "Let us go somewhere else – to the nearby villages – so I can preach there also. That is why I have come." So he traveled throughout Galilee, preaching in their synagogues and driving out demons. (Mark 1: 35-39)

Jesus had to keep going. Yes, people in that town needed Jesus – but He kept going. In the same way, our call is also to keep going – to share God's love with people here, there, and everywhere!

Personal Mission Perspective

Three Things
by Matt Wingert

Jake Youmans has always been the biggest mentor in my life. But it wasn't until I had a couple years of college under my belt that I realized how much he had taught me. I am a constant observer. I observe my peers, my professors, my friends, and my parents. Jake is one of those guys who taught me by example. His life is a giant fishbowl, on display for everyone to see, with nothing hidden. That's how Jake does his ministry – by being genuine and real with the people around him. Jake's life is one *long* mission trip. (Don't let the hair fool you, he is pretty old.) He has taught me many life lessons, but concerning mission trips Jake has taught me three main things that I want to share with you: "Know your audience," "When in Rome, do as the Romans do," and "The mission trip starts the second you get home."

Know Your Audience

It doesn't matter if you are planning the mission trip, or attending it – you have to know your audience. The biggest thing Jake did for St. Paul's Lutheran Church in Orange, California, was to make us a mission-minded church. If we weren't on a mission trip, we were preparing for one. Jake gave us packets and led meetings about the places we were going. We learned about the culture, the economy, the politics, the poverty, and the do's and don'ts – and we PRAYED. After we learned all of that information, Jake had us kids teach the congregation. When leading or attending a mission trip, we are exiting our own culture and comfort zone and becoming a visitor in another. Cross-cultural communication isn't possible without understanding the culture you are going to visit. So read up, and educate yourself about where you are going!

When in Rome, Do As the Romans Do

A part of knowing your audience is experiencing and embracing the culture. It doesn't matter if it's the inner city or the Indian reservation. Experiencing their culture, which is foreign to you, is key to breaking down interpersonal walls and opens up the possibility for them to accept you. When they place food in front of you, eat it. When they offer you water, drink it. I'm not saying throw everything you know about dirty water and undercooked chicken out the window, and I'm not saying sacrifice your dog to the sun, but know that they are watching you just as much as I was watching Jake. If they work until 3 P.M. and then take a lunch break, then you work until 3 P.M. and take a lunch break. If they pray with their hands stretched to the sky, then you pray with your hands stretched to the sky. And most of all – learn the language. (You might look stupid doing it, but who cares.) Experience their culture so you can understand them better. When you base your interactions together off of relationships and friendships, it is so much easier to share the Gospel with them. You and the Gospel will likely be more accepted too!

The Mission Trip Starts When You Get Home

This is the idea of being missional 24/7. Your life is a mission trip. Coming home is the hardest part of the trip. Maybe you saw or experienced some things you want to share that might not be accepted well by your peers, or maybe you just want to spread the love of Christ with people in your community. It could have been a trip to China, or the inner city. Either way, coming home is when the real mission trip starts. For example, time doesn't affect some cultures like it does Americans. Maybe when you get home, you can stop and talk to the homeless man sitting outside of Starbucks for 30 minutes instead of stopping at Panera for breakfast on your way to work. Whatever you learned or were challenged by on your mission trip – take it home to your family and apply it to your life. That is the easiest way to transform your life into a missional 24/7 lifestyle.

All Christians are in a fishbowl. In a world where Christians are becoming a minority, people are watching our every move from the outside. When you leave the parking lot of Zion Lutheran Church in Anaheim, California, there is a sign that reads, "You are Now Entering the Mission Field." This is a reminder of our incredible responsibility and opportunity to shine the light of Jesus to other people in our lives 24/7.

. . . . .

Matt Wingert is a recent graduate of Concordia University, Seward, Nebraska, with a degree in theology and communication. Matt and his newlywed wife, Angela, live in Napa, California, where Angela is an eighth grade teacher. Missions and outreach have always been a huge part of Matt's life. He plans to pursue a master's degree in education, and hopes to become a high school teacher and start a missions program.

Questions from the Crowd

Class is almost over! You're so close to "graduation" and setting off to truly live life as a mission trip. But we have to ask the questions: *What's next? How will my life be different, now that I am living life as a missionary – wherever I am, and in all that I say and do?* As we begin our missional lives, we will also need to be prepared for the questions that others will ask us as we share our faith with them. Let's go back to the early Church and see how the disciples handled these questions from the crowd.

· · · · ·

The Pentecost story found in Acts is one of my favorite stories in all of Scripture. It's the birthday of the "Church." It's the fulfillment of the promise of Jesus that we would receive power – but we had to wait (Acts 1:8). And all of the earth-shaking, wind-blowing tongues of fire, and speaking in the languages of other nations were done in front of a crowd of spiritual people – Jews and converts to Judaism.

The crowd who witnessed the Pentecost experience has always fascinated me. Read the Pentecost story in Acts chapter 2, but this time pay special attention to the crowd, the witnesses of this event. Through the Biblical narrative, the crowd asks four questions that can help us as we look at living life as a mission trip. I believe the "crowd" today is essentially asking the very same questions! But do we have good answers?

The first question can be found in Acts 2:7 – **"Aren't all these who are speaking Galileans?"** This was meant to be a bit of an insult, so translate that – "Aren't all these who are speaking redneck hillbillies?" Galileans were not known for their intellect or insight. And yet note the context given earlier in verse 7; the crowd was **"utterly amazed"** as they asked this question!

Perhaps today, the question that is asked when we share the Gospel is, *Aren't these ordinary, average, common people; how do they have such insight?* When we love others with an uncommon love – people will ask questions. When we share news of eternal significance, not placing ourselves on a higher pedestal but speaking out of humility – people will ask questions. But this question allows us to turn all glory, honor, and praise back to Jesus. Remember that it's not about *you*. It's about Jesus working in you and through you! While I may be ordinary and average, Jesus is not, and that's who I am called to be the "proof" of!

The second question comes in the very next verse, verse 8 – **"how is it that each of us hears them in our native language?"** This is a great miracle in the Pentecost story. The disciples speak, and somehow it's a reverse of the Tower of Babel story in Genesis chapter 11. Everyone hears the Gospel in their own language. They hear it in their vernacular – in a way they completely understand.

Language has power, and as you learned in the Top Ten Ways to Ruin a Mission Trip (in *Missional U*, the first book in this series), learning a person's language allows you to connect in deeper ways. Perhaps today the question is, *Can you tell me in a way I can understand – in a way that will affect my life?* Being missional cannot be abstract. It needs to be concrete and personal. It needs to connect with the individual – in their specific language. In one of my previous books, *Talking Pictures: How to Turn a Trip to the Movies into a Mission Trip*, I talk about this "vernacular" (the language of the people) concept extensively. To be missional, we have to find a way to communicate the Gospel in people's "native" language.

The third question from the Pentecost crowd comes a few verses down in verse 12, where the crowd asks – **"What does this mean?"** This is such a great question! Martin Luther based his entire Small Catechism on this essential question: "What does this mean?" Meaning leads to action and change.

Whenever there is a tragedy, this question comes up. Why did Hurricane Katrina wipe out so much of New Orleans and surrounding areas? Why did a man walk into a movie theater and just start shooting innocent people? Why would two brothers set off bombs at the Boston Marathon? And in a search for meaning, people – who don't even believe in God – start to blame God. In fact, the legal term for a natural disaster is… Act of God! Human beings long for meaning. We refuse to believe that this world and everything we know all happened by accident.

In the movie *Prometheus*, the main characters are searching for the creator. Here is an interesting conversation between David, an android, and a human being named Charlie:[7]

> **Charlie**: What we hoped to achieve was to meet our makers. To get answers. Why they even made us in the first place.

David: Why do you think your people made me?

Charlie: We made you because we could.

David: Can you imagine how disappointing it would be for you to hear the same thing from your creator?

We need meaning! Jesus is **"the way and the truth and the life"** (John 14:6). He gives meaning to life. Our missional life shares this meaning with other people. Our missional life, by the mercy and grace of Jesus, gives people meaning in Jesus!

Now, before we get to the final question from the crowd, let's touch on a particular statement that was made by the crowd. In verse 13 they say, **"They have had too much wine."** It was only 9:00 A.M., so that was perhaps meant to be sarcastic. But the idea of people thinking you are "drunk" or "crazy" because of Jesus is a real issue. People thinking you're crazy is a normal part of the missional life. But notice how it doesn't stop the disciples. They just keep on going. They keep on loving. They keep on sharing. Stopping the loving and the sharing would actually prove the people right! But if we are consistent and live with integrity, the "crazy" argument goes away.

Back to the questions. The final question from the crowd actually comes after Peter's sermon, in verse 37. The people, after hearing Peter's message, are **"cut to the heart"** and ask, **"what shall we do?"**

This is the ultimate compliment in the missional life. When a person asks, *What shall I do?*, they have been convicted by the Holy Spirit and are ready to take the next step in their life with Jesus! We can then remind them that it isn't about what *we* do – it's about what Jesus did for us in living the perfect life that we could never live, dying a brutal death that we would never want to die, and rising again under His own power. What *we* "do" is believe. What we "do" is like cashing a check our father has given us as a gift. We did nothing to earn it, but willingly receive it and thank him for his love!

What shall I do? brings everything full circle. Now the new disciple is called to disciple others. The new disciple is called to be Great Commissional – to live life as a mission trip!

Endnotes

1 (Page 19) *Mission: Impossible II*. Dir. John Woo. Paramount Pictures, 2000. Film.

2 (Page 19) Tim Chester, *Unreached: Growing Churches in Working-class and Deprived Areas*. (InterVarsity Press: Downers Grove, IL, 2012).

3 (Page 22) David Ruis. "Every Move I Make." Every Move I Make. Vineyard, 2004.

4 (Page 54) *Savages*. Dir. Oliver Stone. Ixtlan Productions, 2012. Film.

5 (Page 82) "Who's on First?" Bud Abbott & Lou Costello, copyright 1944. Radio.

6 (Page 151) Martin Luther, "Preface to Georg Rhau's Symphoniae iucundae, 1538," trans. Ulrich S. Leupold, in *Luther's Works: Liturgy and Hymns* (LW), vol. 53, ed. Ulrich S. Leupold (Philadelphia: Fortress Press, 1965) pp. 323–324.

7 (Page 189) *Prometheus*. Dir. Ridley Scott. Twentieth Century Fox, 2012. Film.

I'd love to hear how you're doing on your Missional Too homework! Drop me a line at jacobyoumans@gmail.com. I know God is going to use you in extraordinary ways to advance His kingdom! Know that I am praying for you and I encourage you to be praying for all of the missionaries – around the world and in your backyard! God's richest blessings!

Mailing Address:
    Dr. Jacob Youmans
    Director, DCE Program
    Assistant Professor of Education
    Concordia-Texas
    11400 Concordia University Drive
    Austin, TX 78726

Also from Tri-Pillar Publishing

Life As a Mission Trip

DR. JACOB YOUMANS

Missional Living 101!

Trips to the mission field always bring new spiritual growth and insight to our lives. What if we could learn to see mission not as an event to take part in, but as a lifestyle to embrace? In *Missional U: Life As a Mission Trip*, that's exactly what Dr. Jacob Youmans teaches us as he shows, through Scripture and by personal example, what missional living is all about! If you're looking for a new way to travel, then come along. Missional U is your ticket to an exciting and fulfilling spiritual adventure – one that's sure to last a lifetime!

Dr. Jacob Youmans, a dynamic conference speaker, is Director of the DCE Program at Concordia University in Austin, Texas.

$14.95 – Order online at ww.tripillarpublishing.com

Shaking Scripture

Grasping More of God's Word

Rev. Mark Manning

Shaking Scripture was written to help develop a hunger within you for God's Word. You will see how intriguing and interesting the Bible can be. You will be guided through some of the well-known stories we've grown to love and that have, perhaps, gotten stale with familiarity. In addition, you will discover some lesser-known stories that just might surprise you because of their readability and application. In all, there are 12 devotions, each aimed at "Shaking Scripture" in a way that helps us grasp more of God's Word. Several reflective questions per devotion are also provided, making this book ideal for individual or group study.

Rev. Mark Manning serves as Associate Pastor of St. Paul's Lutheran Church in Orange, CA, where he shares his passion for understanding Scripture.

$14.95 – Order online at ww.tripillarpublishing.com

Abba Daddy Do

exploration s in child like faith

by Dr. Jacob Youmans

Join the adventure of childlike faith!

When you're a child, every day is an adventure! Each day you see and experience life for the very first time. Reclaim the wonder and excitement meant for followers of Jesus as we explore the gift of childlike faith. Jacob Youmans, father of two, walks us through 40 true-life stories, discovering the spiritual in the everyday moments of childhood. Complete with study questions and scriptural references, this book is perfect for the individual looking to grow and be challenged, as well as a family or Bible study group.

Dr. Jacob Youmans, a dynamic conference speaker, is Director of the DCE Program at Concordia University in Austin, Texas.

$14.95 – Order online at ww.tripillarpublishing.com

Powerful Love
An Introduction to Christianity

by Rev. Dr. Lloyd Strelow

You've got questions -
God's love provides the answers!

Powerful Love gets to the core of the essence of our
Christian faith. The first chapter opens the window
to God's love for each of us. It is through that
window - guided by the Holy Spirit - that Christians
see, believe, and live the rest of God's Word.
Throughout Powerful Love, Pastor Strelow uses the
inductive method, using our questions to lead us to
search God's Word and find His answers for faith
and life. Written as a basic guide to the Christian
faith, Powerful Love also includes thoughtful study
questions and an introductory guide

Rev. Dr. Lloyd Strelow has served six congregations in Michigan
and California, including Prince of Peace Lutheran Church (LCMS)
in Hemet, CA, where one of his primary emphases was to teach the
basics of the Christian faith to all who seek to know the Lord.

$12.95 – Order online at ww.tripillarpublishing.com

tALKING PICTURES

*How to turn a trip to the
movies into a mission trip*

by Dr. Jacob Youmans
Foreword by Leonard Sweet

Movies and ministry? What's the story?

Movies are everywhere - at the theater, at home, on
our computers, even in our pockets! Our culture's
fascination with the power of movies brings us
together in a shared experience. But did you ever
think that watching the latest action-adventure flick
with a friend could provide a truly unique opportunity to witness about your Christian faith? Talking
Pictures examines the power of movies in our culture
and explores effective ways in which we can use any
movie as a way to start conversations about our
Christian faith.

Dr. Jacob Youmans, a dynamic conference speaker, is Director
of the DCE Program at Concordia University in Austin, Texas.

$14.95 – Order online at ww.tripillarpublishing.com

Extraordinary News

for ordinary people

by Rev. Heath Trampe

What's so special about being ordinary?

In a world which equates "ordinary" with "not good enough," Rev. Heath Trampe uses powerful examples from the Bible to prove that even ordinary people can accomplish amazing things. As you journey through these 12 stories of inspiration and hope, you'll discover that "ordinary" is a pretty amazing thing to be. This 214-page book includes Bible study questions for each chapter, with in-depth answers and commentary. It is ideal for both individual and group study.

INDIE 2010 NEXT GENERATION BOOK AWARDS FINALIST!

Reverend Heath Trampe graduated in May 2010 with a Masters of Divinity from Concordia Theological Seminary in Fort Wayne, Indiana. Heath is currently serving as Associate Pastor of St. Peter's Lutheran Church in Fort Wayne.

$14.95 – Order online at ww.tripillarpublishing.com

E-DiBS.org
Daily Bible Studies

You're Invited: Study Your Bible, Grow in Christ!

E-DiBS.org is a free online ministry that delivers a brief, video-based Bible study to your personal e-mail address five days a week.

Led by Pastor Paul Stark, sessions are just 8-10 minutes in length and each video is accompanied by a downloadable PDF file for reading or note-taking.

E-DiBS was designed to help people get into the habit of consistent, daily time in the Word of God by removing the two most common barriers that prevent it: lack of time and lack of understanding. With E-DiBS, all you do is point and click, and you're on your way!

- ❖ Learn book by book, chapter by chapter, and verse by verse
- ❖ Share with your friends and family by forwarding the daily e-mail or posting to your Facebook page
- ❖ Great for individual study time, family devotions, small-group ministry, and workplace sharing
- ❖ Search and view 1600+ studies at any time via the Bible Study Archive Page

To learn more or sign up, go to www.e-dibs.org, or drop Pastor Stark a line directly at pillar_ministries@yahoo.com.

CPSIA information can be obtained at www.ICGtesting.com
Printed in the USA
LVOW100027030613

336513LV00001B/4/P